Awakening to the

Sacred Love

of the Twin Flame

D1616401

Awakening to the Sacred Love of the Twin Flame

Shanna MacLean and her Twin Flame, Pra

In honor and memory of my
beloved soul sister,
Yael Hana Powell
1950-2018

I am deeply honored to have the
privilege of continuing to bring your
work on the Twin Flame information to
Earth. I miss you and will love you always.

The minute I heard my first love story,

I started looking for you,

Not knowing how blind that was.

Lovers don't finally meet someone.

They are in each other all along.

— RUMI

DEDICATION

I dedicate this book with deepest Love to my beloved Earth partner, Joseph Amormino. When I first came to know Joseph, I spoke my truth to him: "I can feel your beautiful heart." The spiritual path that we have come to share has been the powerful underpinning for the intimate, loving and giving relationship we experience together every day.

Joseph's patience, generosity of heart, encouragement and his healing talents are all gifts that I have received endlessly. Only an exceptional soul could have walked with me through the emotional pain and illness of my Dark Night of the Soul with the compassion, participation and the understanding that Joseph showed. Only an exceptional soul could have embraced the content of a manuscript such as this book from his partner with excitement and an open mind and heart, receiving Pra unconditionally as a brother and as a part of Shanna.

I am forever in deepest gratitude to Mother Father God for the miraculous blessing of Joseph in my life, and it is because of Joseph's steady support that I am able to offer this manuscript to humanity.

Shanna extends

DEEP PERSONAL GRATITUDE TO . . .

Janice Wolfson—my birthmother—for this incarnation

Millie MacLean—my adoptive mother—for my education

Lumina Croteau—for a Grandmother's Love

Sue, Tony, Tammy—my beloved "children" for their individual beauty and for being my best life teachers

Elora—my spiritual explorer friend

Ingrid Naiman—my first spiritual teacher

Yael and Doug Powell—my Twin Flame spirit family

John Henson—my ever-faithful friend

Robert Conrad—my soul brother

Maria Lazzaro—my pillar of strength sister

Katherine Martel—my hand holding sister

Jane Puryear—my gift from God

Theresa Whitedove—my divine interpreter

Ronna Herman Vezane—beloved teacher and soul family

Joseph Amormino—my beloved Earth partner

Pra—my beloved Twin Flame

My Santa Fe Spiritual Study Groups

Patricia and Meredith—Angels in time of need

Brenda Tompkins—Soul Sister and book Angel

Diane Toups – dearly loved sister and a great heart

Christine Horner—for making *this* book a reality

— and —

Jeshua and Mary Magdalene,

Archangel Mary,

Archangel Michael,

Archangel Raphael,

Masters Adama, Hilarion,

Paul, Saint Germain.

And all my other Masters,

Guides and Teachers

Mother-Father-God,

THE CREATOR OF ALL

Contents

PART ONE :

MY TWIN FLAME

I am at home scanning my incoming emails. I stop at a channeled monthly Message from Archangel Michael via his Sacred Scribe, Ronna Herman Vezane. The title is "The Ecstasy of Sacred Love."

The beloved Archangel posed these provocative questions: "What is it that you yearn for above all things? What is missing from your life that affects everything you think, feel and do?"

He quickly gave the answer: ". . . Sacred Love, dear hearts. We do not mean love as you now experience it in the physical realm, but the Sacred Love of your OverSoul Higher Self, the many Facets of your Higher Self, and ultimately your Twin Flame . . ." [1]

I stopped at those words, **Twin Flame**, as a familiar ecstatic wave traveled through my body. I closed my eyes and watched a delicious "movie" trailer run through my head—snippets of personal experiences from far beyond this world.

It had only been a few years back that those two words, Twin Flame—never before known to me—had become the two most important words in my vocabulary.

Archangel Michael continued: "[Sacred Love] is what you have yearned for ever since you left your lofty home among the stars, and before you divided yourself into two Sparks of individualized awareness—one masculine Spark and one feminine Spark of Divine consciousness—so that you could reflect and experience the glory and diversity of our Father/Mother God.

". . . you have encoded within your DNA and Divine blueprint all the virtues, attributes, qualities and aspects of our Father/Mother God. You are an electromagnetic force field; an energetic package of Divine Light substance.

"Encoded within each of you is the ecstasy and bliss of Sacred Love, a cosmic orgasmic experience beyond anything you can imagine in the physical expression."

And more: "In the past, we have explained how you agreed to separate from your sacred partner in order to fulfill your Divine mission; how you have taken turns in assuming a masculine or feminine body; and how, most often, *one of you stayed in the higher realms while the other incarnated in the physical expression."*

This fit my experience perfectly. One on earth, one on the other side. I resumed my reading.

The Archangel continued: "Rarely were you given an opportunity to meet in the physical world; however, there were wondrous times in the higher dimensions when you were allowed to join together for a time of joyous reunion, for an infusion of loving ecstasy, a blending of your Essence, *a remembrance of what you left behind and what you have to look forward to in the future.* This wondrous gift has not been available to you since you sank into the density of the Third/Fourth Dimensional expression—UNTIL NOW."

Now He had me riveted on His every word.

My mind raced. I thought of all the "Messages from God" about Twin Flames that my beautiful soul-sister and brother, Twin Flames Yael and Doug Powell, had channeled at Circle of Light Spiritual Center, only a few years ago. I had miraculously been called by God to take an active part in this exciting venture. I had helped to bring these magnificent Messages out to the world as administrator of that spiritual center in Eureka Springs, Arkansas. It had been five years since I had left Circle of Light, and since then Yael had returned to our beloved Creator on the other side. I had thought much about that period of my life, and now, suddenly, it was more alive than ever in my mind and in my heart.

Among the Messages from God at Circle of Light, there had been one particular Message called "The SoulMate Dispensation" that seemed parallel, indeed very similar, to what the Archangel was sharing with us now. I quickly looked it up.

Here is a quote: "The SoulMate Dispensation is a magnificent gift from God to humanity. It is a special dispensation that allows SoulMates *to come together before they are in the perfected state of pure Love* that would be the requirement of the natural law of resonance ('like attracts like'). *This means that all on Earth now have access to their SoulMate, their one Twin Flame,* right where they are in their path of awakening." (2)

I later discovered that the Archangel Michael Message that I had been reading was not "new." It had originally been published in 2006 (at which time I had undoubtedly read it), but its message was still very much alive and was being offered again. It was reassuring us that *contact with our Twin Flame, our SoulMate, the other half of us which we had long ago forgotten, was actually available to us now, at this time, on Earth.*

The Archangel's Message continued: "How do you go about connecting with your Twin Flame? First you must say, 'YES TO SACRED LOVE.'

"You must desire this connection with all your Being. You must open your mind and heart to the concept that you have a Twin Flame, and

that it is possible to reconnect with them.

"Are you willing to test this new level of cosmic awareness? Are you ready to accept this Divine gift that is being offered you? Your Twin Flame is waiting for you to put out the call. When you say 'YES to Sacred Love,' *you will feel a dramatic change in your Sacred Heart Center* as it prepares to receive the rarified gift of Sacred Love sent forth from your Mother/Father God. Your earthly life will forever be changed. Call on us and we will guide and assist you in every way possible. I AM Archangel Michael." [3]

Themes from this Message from Archangel Michael played intermittently in my mind and heart for the next few months. Twin Flames . . . Sacred Love . . . Soul Mate dispensation . . .

A little voice seemed to be trying to remind me of something that I wasn't quite ready to hear. It would be a little longer before, one day, I would spontaneously mention to a friend that I thought I might be writing a book . . . And a while after that, I truly remembered in my heart that I had made a promise to continue to bring the Twin Flame information out to the world, and my task was not yet complete.

For most of us, living in a "body" on planet Earth life poses many undesired challenges over a lifetime. As we awaken spiritually, we become ever more aware of the possibility that this is not the only time we have lived, nor the only way we have experienced the phenomenon called "life." We have been gifted with many beautiful reports from sisters and brothers who left this lifestyle through a "near death" experience or other means, and then returned to the solidity of earth bodies to take up once again their "human" role. Almost all of them were wondrously changed and now experienced a much "higher" and loving consciousness. These reports give hope, expand horizons, open us spiritually.

I was one of many earthlings who was given an experience of another way of living and a different experience of Love, so different from what most of us experience on Earth that it changed me forever. You will soon read about my experiences with my Twin Flame which occurred spontaneously. When one has such an experience, it is very necessary to share it! Above all, I have felt the strong desire to encourage everyone to seek the experience that I had, especially since I was told that it IS available to all.

A LITTLE PERSONAL HISTORY

For many, many years, I have been an explorer of the realms beyond daily physical life on Earth.

I have read and listened to an amazing number of spiritual channels, attended many spiritual workshops and read probably hundreds of spiritual books, as I was guided on my spiritual path. I've been animated to explore many extraordinary topics from ETs to life within the center of the Earth to near death experiences.

For a large part of my adult life, I have known in my heart that what we now experience here as life on Earth is *only one adventure*, only one of the multitudinous possibilities open to us, and that at the center of it all is a Grand Source of All Life, most often called *God*, the power of which is Love—what Jesus lovingly called *Abba* (Father).

At a point in my life some time back, I deeply dedicated my life to my passion—"spirituality." I remember speaking aloud, boldly and with strong determination, *"I want to work for God!"*

I meant every word.

BLACK MOUNTAIN, NORTH CAROLINA
2000

Let's go back a little. Of course, we all work for God all the time in one sense, and it wasn't that I felt that my work as an elementary counselor in the public schools in North Carolina was unimportant when I spoke my ultimate desire— to work for God. I felt privileged to serve as an advocate for these little ones in kindergarten through third grade, to teach them life skills and to lighten heaviness in their lives by listening, counseling and helping parents through their challenges.

Sometimes, sitting on the floor talking to a seven-year-old about his parents' divorce while he expressed himself with finger paints, I couldn't believe that this was truly work and that I was being paid to do it! I adored these children. I loved my work very much, and I felt very blessed. Why then would I desire anything else? The answer is that at some level of my being, I was being "called" to something else (I knew not what at that time) just as I have felt "called" right now to share with you what you are reading.

I *can* tell you that before that first "call" materialized, I had no recollection of ever hearing the two words, "Twin Flame," and I considered my male/female relationship life somewhat of a disaster. Three marriages had ended in divorce, and other unproductive encounters had led me to speak to God one day with a strong request. "Please do not bring any more men into my life unless they are given to God and are on a spiritual path as I am." God would take me at my word. It was way over twenty years before I drew to myself another partner in physicality, and he was definitely on my spiritual path.

My spiritual life was my "magnificent obsession." For a long time, I had had a persistent intuitive feeling deep within that there *was* a particular spiritual task waiting for me but I felt a frustration that I had not been able to connect with it.

Then, suddenly, a succession of life events moved me in a new direction. With no warning, the Family Center at my school, an extracurricular project dear to my heart that I had created to support our families, was severely vandalized and rendered unusable. Next, an attempt to renovate my home to help myself feel more comfortable completely backfired. In beginning to prepare the kitchen for new wallpaper, I discovered that all the walls needed to be resurfaced. I lived in dust and confusion for what seemed an endless time and never did get new wallpaper.

The final mysterious event occurred at an evening modern dance performance in the city. I had accepted this invitation to brighten my somewhat reclusive life. The closing dance was a disturbing piece entitled, "Shattered." I remember having an unsettled feeling as the cacophonous music blasted my ears. When I arrived at the parking lot to retrieve my car to drive home, the vehicle had been vandalized and the window had been—yes—shattered. As I waited for the police, I looked up at the sky in a pleading gesture and spoke passionately: "OK, God, I give up! Where do you want me to go and what do you want me to do? Show me!" [4]

Events moved rapidly. Within a matter of a four or five months, by a circuitous route, I found myself as the administrator of a wedding chapel and fledgling spiritual center in Eureka Springs, Arkansas, a place I had *never* imagined being . . . owned by two beautiful new friends, Yael and Doug Powell. I quickly found out that I was definitely "working for God."

Despite a severe disability that had crippled her, Yael "meditated" (as she called her channeling) every day, and brought through a long, handwritten or taped "Message from God." Though I had done little comparable work anywhere in my diverse career life, it soon became evident that I had been brought here to transcribe, edit, and bring these Messages out to the world through a mailing list, published articles and whatever other methods I could devise. Ultimately, I compiled the Messages into many books which we self-published. I also managed the new "spiritual center" and the wedding chapel, taking bookings and arranging every detail of flowers, cakes and decorations. Eventually, I organized Circle of Light workshops to which people came from all over the world. I worked from early morning until late at night every day, and I definitely felt I was living pretty close to my ideal of Heaven on Earth.

How did all *that* happen, you ask? (Remember, I had begged to work for God. Remember, there are no coincidences!) One night, after my car window shattering, I was randomly surfing on the net. I came upon the website of an astrologer whose specialty was finding the optimal location for people on the planet. Feeling guided and having a working knowledge of astrology, I spontaneously asked him to assist me. After interviewing me and examining my astrological chart, he announced that there was only one place within the United States astrologically favorable to my life at this time. It was a small square in the corner of northwest Arkansas. Where??!! I said, with alarm, knowing nothing about the area. He heartily encouraged me, having spent some time in this part of the country earlier in his life. Though a little skeptical, I promised myself that I would have a look.

A seeming obstacle was the fact that I had

already allocated my "schoolteacher summer vacation money" to a spiritual workshop halfway across the country in Reno with Archangel Michael through Ronna Herman Vezane, to whom I have always been drawn. How could I possibly afford another trip? (5)

I remembered that a friend of mine had a friend in northwest Arkansas. This lovely person volunteered to house me so that I could take a look around. Taking a very deep breath, I flew there. *I was exceedingly nervous.* Was this going to be a spiritual wild goose chase? After all, I had a job. What about the school contract I had signed? What about my rented home? Something inside me trembled mightily. Maybe my life was going to change radically? I wasn't sure which viewpoint—staying in the *status quo* or leaping into the unknown—made me more nervous.

I arrived at the home of the "friend of a friend" in Fayetteville, Arkansas, and she had a friend visiting her, who happened to be Yael Powell. Yael rarely left her home because of her physical condition but she had a strong desire to visit her friend because it was Yael's birthday. Spirit is expert at making connections. The next thing I knew I was listening to Yael read one of the Messages from God that she had recently channeled (the topic was Twin Flames). I was astounded at the vibration of this Message and its impact on me. As Yael read, I became mesmerized and felt as though I were floating on the ceiling. The next day, I found myself visiting Yael and Doug at Circle of Light in beautiful Eureka Springs in the northwest corner of Arkansas. We talked for nine hours, and deeply recognized ourselves as the ancient spirit family we are. I committed myself to God on the spot to bring Yael's Messages out to the world. Within a few short months, I had moved there, and the next twelve years brought me utter joy and deliciously hard work.

Many of the Messages from God that Yael was channeling at that time were focused on the topic of Soul Mates, or Twin Flames as it is more often called in Spirit talk. This was completely new information to me. When I returned home to North Carolina to prepare myself for a move, I immediately immersed myself every evening in reading, editing and compiling Yael's Twin Flame Messages for the first book ever published by the spiritual center. It was called, *Say YES to Love, God Explains SoulMates. Very soon, its information would be more than academic to me.*

EXTRAORDINARY ADVENTURES

As I was preparing for my move from Black Mountain, North Carolina to Eureka Springs, Arkansas, I began to have some startlingly unique and completely unexpected experiences. Something I could never have imagined occurred. I was brought together with my Twin Flame in a very unusual way.

It all began with a personal "ah-ha" one evening during meditation. Though I was dedicated to my spiritual growth and expanding my consciousness, I realized that I was very fearful and resistant about relationship. After too many "mishaps" in this area, I had closed my heart. In my meditation, I saw a large metal garage door slide closed, from the top to the bottom—the symbol of my locked-up heart.

Now though, I could feel that things seemed to be changing. The vibration of my new connection with Circle of Light and the power of the Messages from God with their incredible revelations about Twin Flames, my daily read, were having an effect. My heart was being opened!

It was a Sunday evening. Every week at this time, I was accustomed to meditating at 8 p.m. with close friends who lived at a distance. Our intention in our meditation together was the healing of the Earth. Though we lived in different locations, we attuned to each other by phone before beginning. I sat on my usual floor pillow, cross-legged, in my bedroom, near a little table with all my crystals and precious artifacts. I had meditated in this spot for so long that I moved easily into an altered state.

At this time, I followed a guided meditation from Archangel Michael with Ronna Herman Vezane speaking, with a dramatic musical background. The meditation culminated in our entering a beautiful fifth dimensional crystal pyramid. This pyramid had huge crystals projecting from the walls of the interior and a crystal table. It was the apex of higher dimensional beauty and peace. I could see all of this clearly in my inner sight. The pyramid was the sanctuary I would often visit and where I would envision the Earth and its inhabitants being healed and brought to perfection, myself included.

Suddenly, this particular evening, near the end of my meditation, there was a pause in what I was seeing, as though "the movie" of my inner sight had stopped for a moment. The pyramid disappeared, and next, I saw a man, seeming to float in the air in the blank space before me. He was an older man with white hair. He wore a short-sleeved summer plaid shirt and tan trousers, ordinary Earth-looking clothing. His face was weathered-looking. He had high cheek bones, narrow eyes. He seemed very relaxed and seemed to dance around a figure of me. With great surprise, I watched myself floating around with him, and the startling feeling I was having was one of *euphoria*.

At the same time that I was experiencing this in meditation, feeling light years away from my body, my mind back somewhere with my physical body became more than curious. "Who *is* this person and what is he doing here in my meditation?" In my spiritual sight, I saw myself continuing to float around in the air with this gentleman, almost dancing, but not really touching. The feeling was blissful. Then he began to fade away, and I started to come out of meditation.

Now I felt extremely nervous and apprehensive.

Who was this mysterious being? Why was he so old? Some possibilities of people I knew presented themselves, but after considering them, I discarded each one systematically.

Finally, I wondered the thought of thoughts, catalyzed by my reading of all the Circle of Light Messages. "Could this be my Twin Flame?" A powerful intuitive feeling of "yes" surged through me and seemed to be trying to filter through my objections. My little mind began chattering and with it came a full range of feelings. I felt annoyed. This couldn't be my Twin Flame. Twin Flames (Soul Mates) were young and handsome, one's ideal of a partner. This person didn't fit my image of a Soul Mate at all. I didn't like his looks or the way he was dressed. Why was I floating around with him? Why did I feel so comfortable around him? I tried to quell my anxiety about what had just happened and put all of these thoughts out of my mind.

The truth was that these thoughts and sensations were the expressions of fear. I had been closed to relationship, and now, in my sacred meditation, of all places, I had been presented, in this most unusual way, not only with an image of relationship, but maybe with the suggestion of a divine partner. My ego was pulling out all the stops. It took several days to balance myself and come to a place where curiosity and excitement overtook fear and judgment. By next Sunday's meditation time, I couldn't wait to explore what would become an exciting series of encounters that would completely change my life.

* * *

The following Sunday evening, I was preparing as usual for my meditation for the healing of the Earth. During the week, I had received an intuitive message that I should keep notes of any unusual experiences that might occur, and so I initiated what became a habit of always turning on the computer with a blank page set up and ready to type on, before sitting to meditate. That simple act has made it possible for me to share with you the following extraordinary experiences.

As I started the CD for the meditation with the music I always used, I felt the presence of a man standing beside me. He was so real that he was almost but not quite "physical." I sensed him with my eyes open, but when I closed my eyes, he was quite visible in my "spiritual sight." I was startled but excited.

My notes from that evening read: "He looked perhaps in his thirties and wore a brown jump suit as a mechanic might wear to work on vehicles. At first, he was turned sideways, and I saw his profile. I realized it was the same person I had seen in my meditation the previous week. He had the same facial features, only he was much younger. I became tremendously excited and quickly sat down to begin my meditation."

Going on with my notes, "As I moved into meditation, his 'body' was no longer clear to me, but his energy seemed to swirl around me and surround me, always in constant movement. I felt him come very close to me from behind me with his arms around me. Then, he floated very close to my face, almost caressing my face but more as an 'energy' than a physical form. Then, our energies again seemed to 'dance' together in an abstract way, not really touching. All of this was quite thrilling. As his face became clearer to me, I realized that, contrary to my first impressions, he is very handsome! He has a quiet energy, very steady. I saw myself again floating around with him in the space before me. I felt ecstatic and euphoric. It felt WONDERFUL!"

Even though I was seeing and feeling him much more as energy than as a physical form, I felt an incredible familiarity with this being. *I knew him, somehow!* My heart knew the feeling of him. It was as though, all within a matter of a few moments, everything about him was unveiled to me, revealed to me in some mysterious way. I felt his deep passionate commitment to God, a quality of determination about him. His every move seemed purposeful. He had a steady clarity as though he knew what he was doing each moment. I felt a gentle calm about him and a sense of peace. I also noticed that I felt completely at ease and natural with him, *as though I had known him forever.*

My notes continue. "Then came the most

startling moment. Suddenly there we were—
standing in the 'movie screen' before 'me' who
was watching from my sitting position on my
meditation pillow, as though I were looking at a
movie. 'We' were walking down the aisle in what
was obviously a wedding ceremony. I recognized
myself easily, clothed in full wedding regalia, a
long white lace dress with long sleeves and a
train. He was in a tuxedo. We were walking
away from 'the me' who was sitting in
meditation, but we turned around and smiled at
each other and at 'me in meditation' several
times. We looked so blissfully happy! Right out
loud, the 'me' sitting in meditation said, "I can't
believe this!" I was flabbergasted!

"In this Earth life, I have been married three
times without ever making it into a church, or
with any of the ceremonies traditionally
associated with marriage. I WAS SHOCKED! No
other word for it. And yet, he smiled at me as
though I were the only being in his universe, and
I was absolutely radiant. No question about it.
We seemed to be the happiest, most perfect
couple you have ever seen. After that, we were
dancing around again in the air in ordinary
clothing, but I started feeling very 'tired' and
realized I could not stay in meditation any
longer. Reluctantly, I came back."

This second meeting with what I had begun to

acknowledge as my Twin Flame/Soul Mate, in which I was shown, unsolicited and beyond a question of a doubt, who we were together, had a powerful impact on my life. This experience over time began to quietly erase many of my self-doubts, frustrations and self-judgments about myself, especially in relationship to men, and a healing began. I now felt a curious new level of safety and security I had never felt, and I no longer had any interest in participating in male/female relationship adventures in Earth life. I was being given dramatic proof that yes, there was much more to life than the daily "struggles" on this Earth. I felt excitement about giving myself to God in service ever more deeply, as my level of trust accelerated.

This second encounter also set the pattern for recording my experiences with my Twin Flame. When I came out of meditation, I would race for the computer keyboard and type as accurate a description as possible of the experience. I tried to be careful to write exactly what had occurred. I had absolutely no precedent for the experiences I was having, and I can assure you I had no idea at this time of their importance. I shared these by phone with Yael and Doug at Circle of Light, who found them fascinating, but it was many months before I had to courage to share this with anyone else, even my closest friends.

After these contacts in meditation with what seemed to be my Twin Flame, I felt a nervous excitement, wondering what further would manifest and how. Shortly after this meditation visit in which I saw myself as a bride, Yael Powell brought through a long and important channeled "Message from God" at Circle of Light [August 13th, 2000] that greatly expanded our understanding of TwinFlames/SoulMates. During this time, the words SoulMate and Twin Flame were used interchangeably at Circle of Light. I quote from this Message:

"Your SoulMate is not some random being whom you might find if you are lucky. You *will* find your SoulMate. You cannot *not* find your SoulMate for you ARE your SoulMate and your SoulMate is you. Yes, you are individuals. And you are not. For as I have told you, you are two parts of one cell in My heart. Nothing can keep you apart.

"Now, as Creation moved—outward, inward and multidimensionally—each cell of My heart, each of you as SoulMate pairs, also burst forth in an explosion of joy and excitement that seeded yourselves all the way along the path of individualization. In other words, you placed pieces of yourselves along the way. <u>The goal was for you to gain enough individuality that you could live within Me, but not merge your consciousness with Me.</u>

"Now I Am calling you Home. It is time to recognize your own heart. Nothing can keep you from each other. It is a requisite of your opening heart. *In truth, you are one.* Once you get to the point of real access to your heart, you will see your SoulMate." [6]

It was some time into the future before I began to understand the true content of this Message from God, but the seeds were being sown in my curious intellect. ". . . you ARE your SoulMate and your SoulMate is you." I will refer back to this and many similar Messages throughout this story, as I explore our true origins, our birth from our beloved Creator to our complex adventure in physicality, and *what we are touching when we reunite in any way with our beloved Twin Flame.*

* * *

My next meditation with my Twin Flame was perhaps the most emotional moment of my life, and it moved our relationship to a new level of intimacy and communion. As it unfolded, I again sat in meditation, watching the kaleidoscope of rapidly moving pictures on the screen of my inner vision. It was like watching and being in a movie at the same time, a movie with elements of both Earth life and the ethereal streams of otherworldly energy. At the same time, I experienced the feelings—and what feelings!

There was certainly very clear and perfect divine purpose in the unusual way Spirit chose to present my Twin Flame to me. Since, as with most of us on Earth, I had forgotten that my Twin even existed, how could I possibly have understood what these encounters in meditation represented—unless I had experienced him within my spiritual sight at the same time that I could feel him in my heart and throughout my energy field. It is now clear to me that had I met him in a physical body in ordinary Earth life, I might not have "recognized" him, given the limited information I had about Twin Flames at that time. Recently, I asked Pra why he came to me in this way—in spirit during my meditations. He made clear that this was the most expedient way for me to gradually comprehend who he was and what was occurring—so that I could be a messenger through this experience for others on Earth.

So, our meetings were unveiled before me in the symbols of the Earth world like a movie and seemed to be occurring somewhere between physical life on Earth and higher dimensional consciousness. We were shown wearing bodies and clothing and participating in activities that we all know on Earth, as well as activities in the higher realms. However, in this "bridge world," the energy was much higher than on Earth, so the events before my eyes were always fast‑moving and displayed in constantly changing snippets and flashes.

Now, from the vantage point of time lapsed and wisdom gained, I realize how amazing was this gift I was given of these meetings with my Twin Flame. I also realize that this reunion was presented as it was because it had been one of my soul purposes for this lifetime to bring the remembrance of this information about the Twin Flame to humanity. Why else was I magnetized to Circle of Light and the Twin Flame Messages from God? The book you are reading is a further fulfillment of the main purpose for which I incarnated. But how would I have known such a thing at that time?

Here are my notes, written immediately after our powerful third meeting.

"I started the guided meditation and music I always used and sat to meditate. I felt myself going 'up.' On the movie screen of my inner vision, I saw myself being pulled up a vertical rope, exactly the way tight rope artists ascend to their bar at the circus—lifted up swiftly with my arm outstretched, dressed in some kind of leotard. This was one of many symbols used to indicate 'ascending' to a higher vibration.

"My Twin Flame was there and took my hand, and we whirled in an amazing dance, sort of a combination of ballet and ballroom. I couldn't see his face very well, just our figures together, then the tremendous sweep of soft energy, very soft and peaceful . . . a constant gliding feeling. We whirled and whirled. There are beginning to be energetic qualities I recognize about him. He is always very peaceful, serene—yes, serene is the right word. He has a marvelous calm, and yet, he's very clear and sure of every next move.

"A series of vignettes, quick scenes followed. He took my hand and we stood face to face. These scenes flickered in and out, and once again, his face was not always clearly visible to me. It was a communication of hearts, and it seemed that we were sharing feelings for each other. He very gently kissed my face and took my hand and led me to a bench where we sat facing each other for a while, again communing silently.

"Then he led me to another place where we could see mountains in the distance, very big mountain peaks, pastel-colored, bathed in a beautiful diffuse light. Walking, we came to a 'cliff,' and the next thing I knew, we were FLYING! He had my hand, and we simply flew through the air, without any device or effort, I along beside him, or slightly behind him. At one point, he put his arm around my waist to support me, and at another point, carried me in his arms.

"As I write this at the computer, I am unable to stop sobbing, which is how I know it is TRUE—that it actually happened. I feel as though my whole being has been opened in a way I can't describe. Emotion pours from me. I have never in my life had such feelings. It is hard to type. I still feel very much 'out of my body' but I so want to save this that I am forcing myself to write it, despite tears and fuzziness.

"We flew for a while and suddenly we were on a 'platform' in the 'sky.' It seemed to be simply suspended there, very large. I thought it might be some kind of a 'spaceship' as used in interstellar travel, but I didn't see anything like a ship—just a platform that seemed to have no beginning or end. We sat down on what seemed to be soft green grass amidst some trees and flowers that looked more or less like the kind we have on Earth. We held hands and looked into each other's eyes in a silent reverie.

"Pra (that seems to be his name—Pra. I'm not

sure how I know this. Did he tell me?) said, 'Look!' (all communication was telepathic), and suddenly it was dark, and we were sitting right in the middle of a dark night sky that was overflowing with stars. They were everywhere, above us, beside us, under us, and all sizes. It was very dark, and we were close, oh, so close to them. They were right there and shone like tremendous lights all around us. I was totally overwhelmed, looking from one side to another in complete amazement. I wasn't sure where to look first. It was all so brilliant around us.

"We sat there together for a while, holding hands. Then, the sky seemed to be getting lighter. Pra signaled me to 'come,' and I took his hand. We took off flying again for quite a while through the night, still filled with stars. Then, something very glittery began to appear in the far distance, and I began to see a mammoth crystal 'city'—large tall crystalline structures, clusters of them, HUGE, like great sentinels, and below them, areas of luscious meadows and green vegetation, with some low mountains far in the distance. It was all so beautiful, beyond words, luminescent, sparkling, vibrant, sending off a radiation, making the air seem full of champagne bubbles. Pra stopped and turned to me. I heard the words audibly, 'This, Beloved Shanna, is our Home.'

"I began to weep so much that I am unclear as to what happened next. As I write this, I am still sobbing. It was as though every feeling I was holding in my heart from my whole life opened at that moment. We went further past the huge crystals to green meadows, and we landed and stretched on the ground on a grass carpet. We held each other and communed with each other heart-to-heart in a way that wasn't very physical. I was crying and crying. The extraordinary beauty of the setting, the bliss of being with Pra, the idea of 'home'—it was all too overwhelming for me. Pra seemed to understand, and he was very comforting.

"After a time, we left again in flight, and things became very vague after that. I do remember looking back at those huge gorgeous sparkling crystal columns. We came to some place that felt more like where I had previously met him. I realized he was leaving. I felt so emotional that I began to cry again, as he faded to my right, blowing kisses to me. I asked telepathically, 'Will I see you again?' I received his answer, 'Yes.' 'Will you come into the physical and be with me, and do our work together?' I begged. I couldn't bear the thought of leaving him. Then, I heard the whispered words, 'Have patience, Beloved. All will come to pass.'

"I was again sobbing by then and telling him

over and over how much I wanted to be with him. Now as I write this, I can't stop crying uncontrollably. It was such an intense and amazing experience emotionally that I don't yet know where to put it. Despite all this emotion, I feel very happy that I was able to record all of this. I am starting to come back into the body. I notice that this whole encounter took about half an hour."

This third visit with my beloved Twin Flame, Pra, and his reference to our "home" touched me in the deepest recesses of my heart and awakened the remembrance in me of who we are together. I had never in my entire life experienced such emotion. My heart, my whole being was opened. My body was overwhelmed.

In this present lifetime, I chose to come into embodiment as an adoptee—to experience the trauma of being given up for adoption at two weeks old, after being breast fed by my mother who was unable to keep me. I was adopted into a family that did its best amidst alcoholism, gambling addiction and financial instability. Fears of abandonment and insecurity have travelled with me throughout this incarnation. The reference to "Home," articulated by my Twin Flame—suddenly revealed in this unique way at a level of feeling so much deeper than I had ever experienced—broke down all my emotional defenses. At the same time, the depth and purity and the eternal quality of our Love flooded through my being. My "Home," of course, was with him in God and always had been.

These visits with Pra, all occurring in the setting of my meditation time, took place over five months, and there were about thirty of them, all variations of what I present here. I have selected certain of these moments to share with you, the reader, so that you may have the flavor of these powerful experiences. Here are my notes captured on the computer the following Sunday evening that found me more ready than ever for another meeting with my beautiful, yet enigmatic, Twin.

"I saw myself walking up a long flight of stairs in the outfit I had worn that day: a purple flowered silk skirt and my favorite white sweater. Pra caught me in his arms and twirled me around, and there was some dancing and silent communing. He looked exactly as he had the past few times we have met—young, handsome, short hair, tall and thin. Sometimes I saw his 'uniform' in the flashes on the screen before my eyes. This looked somewhat like a military dress uniform, like a 'space commander'? Perhaps this was one of his manifestations. It was navy blue with a red and gold striped band at the neck.

"We walked with arms around each other into a dark background like the night sky and a big display of stars. We weren't standing on anything, just walking on 'nothingness.' We were very easy and natural together, just very happy to be together.

"Then I asked him (all telepathic through pictures and thought forms) to go to the meditation for the Earth with me (what used to be my Sunday night gig). He said, "Of course," and we floated to the Crystal Pyramid. My meditation friends were already there. When I walked in with Pra, everyone applauded and made jokes and laughed. He smiled and was very gracious. We just looked at each other, grinning.

"We stayed a short while, but then Pra took my hand, and we exited top right of the movie screen in my spiritual sight and were in the star-filled night scene again. We flew, and from my vantage point on my meditation pillow, I could clearly see my violet flowered skirt fluttering in the breeze. We came to what looked like an enormous spiral made up of stars, high up above us, against an endless black backdrop of a dark starry night. Pra explained that this was the StarGate, and I think he said that there would be a strong pull because of the magnetic forces there. [7]

"He was very animated describing many things about the StarGate that I did not quite understand. We flew around it and viewed it from different angles. He held my right hand in his left hand, gesturing with his right hand and explaining with great enthusiasm. Then, Pra showed me that the two of us, arms around each other's waist, were standing at the entrance to the StarGate, welcoming brothers and sisters who were arriving. This was very exciting! [Sometimes we would appear in more than one place simultaneously in my meditations.]

"We flew to some other places in the cosmos—places that looked like the night sky but sometimes had planets or balls of light. He said telepathically that he was giving me a tour of the region. We passed a place that had mountains colored like rainbows. Then we were zipping back to the Earth meditation. When we entered, a friend asked me the question: 'Where were you?' I said, 'We went for a walk.'

"The Earth meditation was finished, and Pra and I then began a long dancing sequence. We twirled in an old-time movie (Ginger Rogers and Fred Astaire) act with fancy dancing and much laughing and silliness. I had a tremendous feeling of euphoria, and my physical body (sitting in meditation, watching) laughed and laughed. It was very fun. There were close communing moments, too. Very clear. I could see both of us clearly.

When I am with him, nothing else exists. Being in his energy is just completely blissful, and I feel endless ecstatic waves of love, love, love. I adore him and I feel so adored.

"Then I got a signal that it was time to come back. I asked Pra telepathically to come back with me, and we descended very slowly hand-in-hand down a stairway. I could feel the slow descent in my body, a little like air slowly being released from a balloon. At one point he picked me up from behind with his hands around my waist and carried me a few steps, with both of us laughing. He came all the way back with me and sat beside me in my room to my right as I slowly came back into my body.

"When he was sure that I was back safe and sound, he flew off to the right, blowing me a kiss. I watched him go and we waved from a distance. Oh, the miracle of Pra . . . miracle, miracle, miracle. Oh, the miracle of Love . . . Oh, that these feelings would be everywhere on Earth. I gave deepest thanks to Mother-Father-God for this most extraordinary experience. I felt calm and so, so joyous inside."

Throughout all these meetings in meditation setting with my Twin Flame, the multimedia quality was consistent. I would "feel" his energy around me very strongly, encompassing my physical body and the energy field extending from me for quite a distance. This sometimes gave me a buzzing, lightheaded intoxicated kind of feeling. I felt as though hundreds of butterflies had been released in my chest and stomach. All of this was the power of the magnetism between us, and the adjustment of the dense physical body to the powerful and extraordinary Love vibration that was being poured to me from higher dimension.

At the same time that I was having the energetic experience, I would consistently watch through my spiritual sight, symbols or pictures of us interacting with each other, exactly as though we were in a movie being played out in color upon the big screen before my eyes. The main difference between this and a traditional movie was that it lacked the continuity of continuous images. Instead, I saw us often less than solid, more as in our light bodies (although we wore earth clothing), flickering in and out, and the settings changed rapidly. It seemed we were always in motion.

As I learned to adjust to the higher vibration of our meeting places, I experienced continuous waves of ecstatic bliss and often euphoria throughout our meetings. I would laugh as though I were infused with laughing gas. At times, I would shout for joy, totally incredulous at how happy I was feeling.

The reader may recall that during the time of these early visits with my beloved Pra, I was still working as a school counselor in North Carolina. During the week, I arose at 5:30 a.m. to get to my post at school by 7:15 a.m. As a counselor, my days were taken up with all manner of human problem-solving that on the surface seemed completely "unspiritual." But even at school, I silently invoked the angels for blessings for the children and to bring Love to each and every situation. Sometimes when I had a parent meeting, I would call Pra ahead of time to clear the air in my office and fill the room with blessings and Love vibrations. When I felt the need of time for centering during the day, I visited the "meditation room," the only place where there was relative silence and peace in a busy elementary school—the bathroom.

The Pra visits were beginning to extend to more evenings than Sundays. I felt that I was leading a double life, especially since I shared these experiences with no one except by phone with Yael and Doug.

On the following Thursday evening, I met my Twin at 7 p.m. in our usual manner—during my meditation. I want the reader to know that these notes I am inserting about my visits with Pra *are* the verbatim notes from the moment of the experiences and provide the way I am now able to recapture the freshness of such an amazing adventure.

"SO, SO EXQUISITE! I have a big smile on my face! I don't know whether I can remember the exact order of things as there is no 'time' in the higher dimensions, and one image seems to flow into another, sometimes bumping into each other. I went upward faster and faster, and I raced into the arms of my beloved with big hugging and kissing. Then there was flying (we LOVE to fly) arms around each other, sometimes with our wings, sometimes not. Sometimes I just hang on to him, and he leads me. We looked at stars and flew all over the starry night.

"We created a beautiful vision of Earth together, sending Love out from our joined heart to humanity. I sighed to Pra, 'Oh, if only we can use this Love we feel for everyone on the planet.' And again, we envisioned this happening and the power of all of our Twin Flame Love going out to all these people. Sometimes we placed an image of the Earth within our Twin Flame heart, and I covered it with little hearts—our Love. Or, we would place a group of people in our heart, or a country, or a continent. Thinking of using this gift I have been given, this miraculous Love, for the benefit of others is so very thrilling to me. Of course, Our Beloved Creator would give us such beauty for each of us in a form that we would be giving to others as well! I am just beginning to learn about all the ways Pra and I can use our Love for bringing more Love to the Earth.

"Then, there was a long and delicious ice-skating sequence. It was exactly like a performance in the Olympics. Pra and I were skating across the sky with routines that would rival the winners of the Olympics. I wore a light lavender skating outfit, and of course, I had a perfect skater's figure. Pra was his usual handsome self (he REALLY is!). The ease with which we moved was fabulous. Pra shows himself to me as tall and thin, and he is tremendously gentle and graceful in all that he does. I couldn't believe some of the leaps and turns and routines we performed.

"There are no 'mistakes' with Pra. He knows exactly what he is going to do every minute. There are never misplaced steps or a lack of grace. Dancing, flying and now skating are some of our favorite activities. We did extraordinary leaps and jumps tonight. It's pretty easy in higher dimensions with no gravity, and it is very delightful! Every now and then we would come together for a hug. The most fun part was just skating, arms around each other, looking into each other's eyes, in absolutely perfect harmony.

"Then we took a flying trip to the StarGate and flew around it, looking at it from various viewpoints. As previously described, it is a deep, deep spiral made of stars. Then the two of us stood at the StarGate to the right of the opening, and Pra pointed for me to look into the distance. What I saw were what seemed like hundreds of couples walking together in a winding trail through the starry night, making their way slowly to the StarGate. It was an astounding sight.

"I looked at Pra with the question, 'Twin Flames'? He nodded yes. The line went on 'forever.' As they passed into and through the StarGate, I looked to see what happened, and I saw them flying with arms around each other exactly as Pra and I do. Wow! I asked Pra telepathically, 'Are they free? Do they now know freedom [from earth life]'? He nodded with a smile. 'Yes. Now they are completely in God's Love.'

"Finally, I felt Pra telling me that it was time to go back. I protested but he quietly and gently started taking me back (he has a way of making hard things easy) and we dropped slowly like two leaves in the breeze, and then he held me, and we continued downward together. I asked him telepathically if he would come all the way down with me. I said I didn't want to leave him, and he said that he never leaves me and that we are together forever, for eternity.

"I came down from the higher realms very easily tonight and came into my body quite gently. A few hugs and Pra was off into the air to my right, waving. Then he circled as he often does, in front of me, both of us waving, and then he went up, up, up and I finished coming through my crown, down into my body, fully."

* * *

During this period when my counseling work in North Carolina was drawing to a close and I was preparing to move to Circle of Light in Arkansas, I spent my evenings reading and editing

Messages from God which Yael had sent. We had promised (God) to get a first book of the Messages into publication as soon as possible, and this was very much in process at a distance. I had all of the Messages on the topic of Twin Flames/SoulMates that had been sent by fax, spread out on the living room floor in piles, and I was using my guidance to select which ones would appear in the book and in what order. I later learned that my silent partner, Pra, was the best source of this kind of information and much more. Later, at Circle of Light, he guided many of our activities, especially workshops, with messages given through both Yael and me.

I had also been feeling quite ill with a kind of flu, not uncommon when one overworks and when one works with small children. Here are my notes from an unexpected visit from Pra.

"This evening I went out for the first time since feeling ill to buy food. When I got in the store, I realized that Pra was shopping with me. This made me feel very shaky and disoriented (I know he was just watching over me), and I felt uneasy that I had gone out before my body was ready. I accomplished what I needed to quickly and came home. Pra urged me to go right to bed.

"I lay down in the bed and felt Pra's energy there beside me. My body was very tired and feeling very weak. I kept on yawning and yawning. I felt him stroking my head, all of this on the energetic level, but some of it could almost be felt in the physical. He was 'snuggling' with me. I took the pillow and allowed it to be a 'body' for him, and experienced the most loving, gentle, nurturing, protective, pure energy. He finally did help me to go to sleep, although I wanted to be awake to feel him on every level.

"When I awoke about 4 a.m., I called for Pra. The next few hours were spent in the most indescribably exquisite, precious 'tantric' joy. I say 'tantric' because it is the only comparable Love Making on Earth in which one can feel the complete range of ecstasy with minimal physical touch. I experienced what it felt like to give and receive totally of my and his being, energetically. At one point, I talked to him about the fact that my physical vehicle wanted him to be in a physical vehicle so that I could experience on that level as well. Perhaps that will be possible, although I doubt it could approximate what we experienced together this morning. It was wave after wave of Love and tenderness and exchange and the gentlest, almost-touching waves of heart opening, treasuring each other, unspoken adulation for each other, sending back and forth waves and waves of Love. So ecstatic and euphoric. Yes, orgasmic! We do not seem to have many words in our language for these feelings.

"I felt as though I could stay there with him forever. Sigh! I had no plan to write this, but then I realized that nothing about our lives is personal any more, and who knows its future use. So I explained to Pra that though these were the most precious moments of my life to me, I still had to record it." He agreed.

Despite the illness of my physical body, I had a magnificent visit with Pra at our usual time on the following Sunday evening. The condition of my body did not seem to affect my ability to operate in the higher dimensions. Here are my notes:

"On the way up, I was deciding my wardrobe for the visit, as I didn't want to look at myself in my old pajamas for an hour as happened the last time. I chose my rose-colored velvet top and gray silk pants. I went up by swimming, just as you would in a pond or at the ocean. I started out slowly with the crawl stroke but as I swam, I got faster and faster near the top and swam (ran) into Pra's arms. There is such a magnetic pull between us.

"I have never in my deepest imagination even dreamed of such feelings of Love and attraction and bliss and euphoria and perfection for another being.

"I am beginning to understand what I have read in Yael's channeled Messages from God . . .

what God means when He/She tells us that our Twin Flame mirrors God's Love for us, His/Her children. In the Messages, God explains that the Twin Flame relationship is God's gift to us of God's Love. We can have relationship with God— what is called 'the one degree of separation' that allows us to 'know,' 'perceive' God, rather than simply be merged with God in the great ocean of Love. In the same way, *though we are one being with our Twin, we can have the 'one degree of separation' that allows us to feel and perceive each other and know through the heart the bliss of Twin Flame Love.*

"Tonight we skated some, and I suddenly acquired a short gray skating skirt instead of my silk pants. We did some absolutely incredible (that's the right word!) skating routines tonight. We also danced close a lot, my head on Pra's shoulder, because he is a lot taller than I. Anyway, touch dancing. Slow and huggy. Then, we walked in a woods that had some autumn leaves, hand-in-hand, eating apples. At the end of the woods was a cliff into nothingness, and we took off flying into the star-filled night—an endless darkness lit by gorgeous lights, the stars.

"We began communing about the nature of all of this. I asked Pra more about the higher dimensions. He responded telepathically that we can have whatever we want here. So, we tried taking turns having thoughts and feelings and watching them immediately manifest. We went to a beach, stretched in the sun, then jumped around in the ocean. We had an ice cream sundae at a little table with a white tablecloth and white napkins. Pra had to eat with his left hand because we didn't want to let go of holding hands. I got the full realization that in the higher dimensions, you just think it!

"Then I asked Pra about 'beyond.' Would we always be together? Would God decide that we were no longer the two who were one, and join our energies back into the sea that is God Love, and would we lose each other? Pra said we would always be the two who are one. I asked if we would ever be 'separated' again. Pra said no. If we were sent somewhere, it would be together. I asked about what we would do when I completed the Earth assignment.

"Suddenly the whole question of the next phase of God's creativity was on my mind. I know that Pra told me a lot here, and that my consciousness absorbed it, but I can't quite relate it through my little mind. We were walking now, holding hands, and he was 'talking' very intently to me with that concentrated, serious expression he gets when he is explaining something. I saw myself listening with a look of attentiveness.

"I know that a part of the conversation had to

do with assignments from God. Pra was saying that if God suggests an assignment, because we are One With All, if there is some way we can be of service, of course we desire to do it. There are many 'places' we could be 'sent' in service, and it is impossible to know what they might look like or where they might be. God creates infinitely.

"Then I saw us as two HUGE beings, made of light? cloud? Whatever it was, we were formless, but two little hands were observable in the midst of the massive expanse of light, and we were still holding hands. We floated, totally filling the sky. I was feeling like getting my Pra back and having a hug (after all, I had just reunited with him two months or so before), so that's just what happened.

"We were back dancing close and being affectionate. Somehow dancing evolved into going home (darn!) and he was dancing me downward and hugging me at the same time. I asked him if he would come back with me. He said he would visit later. We held hands coming down to a certain point, and then I went alone. Pra waited until I was back in the body, then waved and flew upward. I asked, 'Thursday? Maybe before? Will you surprise me?' He liked that, a big YES."

* * *

Everything that was shown to me visually during the meditations had a symbolic meaning. You may recall that I was quite convinced that there was no partner for me on Earth, an irony indeed in view of all that happened later, but at that time, I had closed my heart to any possibility. Pra's first appearance, therefore, brought him in a form that I would find "unattractive." As I opened my heart to the possibility of my Twin Flame, Pra appeared ever more physically attractive in my meditations—taller, younger and ever more handsome.

Every part of the visual aspects of these visits was a symbol. It is our understanding that the realms of Love are without physical form, more like streams of light. In my meetings with Pra, we were shown flying, dancing and skating— everything was very fast moving but we wore the clothes, the garments of Earth life. This was God's magnificent gift to me that I might reunite with my Twin Flame, who was not at this time in physical form, in a way that I could gain enough understanding at this point in my "awakening" to be a messenger for others.

The wings carried me from Earth life to Pra's domain. Wings have always been a symbol of angels and higher dimensional beings—access to a "higher" reality. Often a stairway or an escalator would appear when it was time to go "home," depicting descent from the rarified atmosphere of my travels into the denser vibration on Earth. These stairways were a marvel in their variety—the long descending stairs resembling government buildings in Washington, D.C., or many variations of rock or slate stairways or passageways through woods with ponds and grottos for resting places. However delightfully they were depicted, a stairway meant "going down," "going back home".

The wedding scene, shown to me immediately in the second visit, was a confirmation for me in the symbols of Earth life of the truth that this WAS my eternal divine partner. I had always been "married" to him, and in the realms of light we were in bliss together. When we visited the place Pra called "Home," the magnificent crystalline clusters radiating emanations of sparkle, I initially thought this was a specific place in the cosmos (which it may have been) but I came to understand that this was symbolic of our Real life in consciousness—the pure creative essence of streams of Love that we are, in the truth of us. We are truly beings of consciousness.

The Infinity symbol—the figure eight on its side—is the classic symbol of eternity, evoking the never-ending cycles of creation in which the Twin Flames are God's representatives. It is often used to represent the Twin Flames. Frequently, Pra would use the Infinity sign in contacting me, moving my hand or my fingers in the shape of an eight; or we would fly in the shape of figure eights in the sky.

The StarGate and its pathway symbolize the return of humanity to its original state of pure Love—the opening of hearts. As each being would come into reunion with his/her Twin Flame, the Twin Flames would fly through the symbolic StarGate. This was a symbol of their freedom from the confines of Earth life into the life of the Spirit, now as streams of light, on their "way back to" God.

As I reread my notes and ponder which of these approximately thirty miraculous visits to share further with you, the reader, it is a difficult decision.

I wish for every brother and sister on earth to make contact with his/her Twin Flame, and the way to do it is to know the beauty that you are and hold the vision and the DESIRE in your consciousness.

Though we often forget this in our daily earth life, "we are children of God." We are made in the image and likeness of our Father, our Creator, and we have great co-creative capacities. Our desires do manifest. So, as I look over these accounts of my visits with my Twin, Pra is telling me to "share abundantly."

Here is another blissful and euphoric visit with my Twin Flame.

"I went up like a leaf blowing upward in the wind. Pra was there and held me tight against his chest. We started flying and found ourselves in a forest. Pra led me to a place under lovely pine trees where there were pine needles on the ground, and we lay down, embracing. All of a sudden, the place was alive with 'little people.' They came from everywhere. Devas, fairies, elementals, all kinds of them. We were in the middle of their 'downtown.' Pra seemed to know them all well and seemed not surprised. I, of course, was completely agog. They were so friendly and loving.

"Then, animals came out from everywhere to greet us and gathered around us. A deer was licking Pra's cheek. As we got up and took a walk along with them, the forest just filled with wildlife, like a scene from a Walt Disney movie! When we got to the edge of a precipice, we waved goodbye and started flying.

"We landed in the most heavenly site, a gorge through the mountains with old growth trees and everything crystal pure and untouched. We marveled at the view and then dropped down to a flowing river below. There was a raft conveniently waiting with two cushions, and we floated down this river for quite a while, hugging and enjoying the incredible bounty of Nature. It looked like a visionary painting. Then, we came to a waterfall, but Pra jumped off holding my hand before we got to it, and we were flying again.

"There was much Love Making tonight with our light bodies joined and all of the chakras lit, flying in the Infinity sign and tremendous explosions of firecracker-like displays as we twirled together in the 'sky.' It was very dramatic and certainly answered any questions I might have had about the subject of Love Making. My physical vehicle can still feel it! During all of this, I felt INTENSE EUPHORIA, absolutely incredible.

"I asked Pra telepathically, 'Are we Making Love without bodies?' He laughed and laughed, and I got a tremendous YES for an answer. Whew! We ended with figure skating, tremendously fun, fancy jumps and twirls, always stopping for hugging and kissing. It took a long time to come back tonight. We came down a stairway, but it seemed that there was a skating pond at every few steps, and we would go back to skating. There was so much reluctance to leave each other. Finally, he made his characteristic gesture that he does when he is leaving (he turns his body away from me and starts upward) and then he crossed in front of me through the 'sky.' I came back very slowly, and when I landed solidly in my body, I started laughing wildly and screaming and yelling with joy. I had so much energy. Even now, I can't get the smile off my face. HEAVEN! HEAVEN! HEAVEN!"

* * *

Although I did not know it, my very frequent and incredible visual visits with Pra in the higher dimensions during meditation were approaching a close. As I prepared to move to Circle of Light, another phase of our extraordinary relationship was waiting to open. But, before that happened, a week later, I had another unforgettable experience, so sweet and beautiful that I just have to share it with you. It was recorded as follows:

"Gosh, it went by so quickly! I can't believe it's been an hour. I went up as usual and met Pra with many hugs and kisses. He was wearing his 'StarGate uniform,' dress 'military' and very handsome. He picked me up and twirled me around a few times, then motioned, 'Come,' and we were flying.

"Pra said, 'There is a place I want to show you.' Next we were hiking in huge mountains (turned out to be the Himalayas) that were completely covered by snow. Logic would say that it was cold there, but we were comfortable. I had on jeans and a white cotton shirt, and Pra had "changed" to something casual. We were climbing on a path that seemed to me to be very steep. I complained a little, and Pra picked me up as though I were a feather and carried me in his arms. That was nice for me, and I took advantage by throwing my arms around his neck and kissing him frequently.

"We came to vegetation and what seemed like a hidden monastery. There was a gate covered in vines, and a monk greeted us and let us in. Then we walked a flowered path into the most beautiful, completely natural place. There were many monks there in long Franciscan-type robes, and they all seemed to know Pra well. He stepped forward and embraced them one-by-one. Then he presented me. "This is my beloved Shanna." One-by-one, they embraced me warmly as well. They were the most peaceful, beautiful people, and this place had a tremendously high, calm energy—peace beyond peaceful. There were many scenes here—rapidly changing snippets— us in their vineyard picking and eating grapes, admiring their beautiful vegetable gardens, being introduced to their animals, me playing with the baby goats.

"Then they showed us to a very austere bedroom where we stayed (there was a bed and a single candle on a simple dresser). We sat with them at meals and sat in meditation and prayers with them several times a day. It felt as though we stayed there several days. I asked about the place, and Pra said, "This is a place where many Masters have come to study.' The word 'study' was said with Pra's bemused look, giving me the idea that the kind of study one did here was not the usual kind. As we were walking with the monks, I saw Jeshua (Jesus) several times . . . a quick flash of his embodiment in a form known to us on Earth, as though his energy were there. I asked Pra, and he confirmed that yes, Jesus had 'studied' there.

"'When we left, they all embraced us again with their most heavenly energy, and we started down the mountain path. We walked only a little way when Pra said, 'Why walk?' and we were in the air, flying. I was looking at Pra and thinking how wonderful he is and what wonderful places he takes me, and of course, he picked up my thought form immediately, and in-the-air LoveMaking ensued!

"There were many other brief segments this evening. We were dancing ballroom style, very slowly and romantically, and I had on a dark, full length velvet dress, very beautiful. Then, we were way, way up in the sky flying, intertwining and becoming like a comet. We flew in 'Infinities' (figure eights) in all directions, and Pra wrote 'Pra loves Shanna' in skywriting (in cursive, as the kids would say) which we then flew in and out of as it slowly dissolved. MUCH FUN!

"Suddenly we were in a city, walking down a long, long flight of steps that seemed part of a building. We were in city clothes. Pra was wearing a long tweed coat, looking like a lawyer, his New York City coat is the way I think of it, and I also had on my tweed winter coat. We were hand in hand and chatting and having fun, but I realized WE WERE GOING DOWN. It is amazing all the guises that this can take. When we got to the first landing, there were hugs and kisses and another flight of steps together, but I knew at some point that I was going down and he wasn't. That is, of course, what happened with the usual 'waving, throwing kisses' ending.

"When I came back, I had a very quietly happy feeling—the many emotions when with

Pra, all of them WONDERFUL! He is always in constant joy, sometimes quiet and sometimes more animated, but always joyous and that is what I always feel around him. I feel such awesome gratitude for Pra, beyond any words I could find to express it. The gift of my life!"

CIRCLE OF LIGHT
January 2001

I'm here in Eureka Springs, Arkansas at Circle of Light Spiritual Center, and I'm excited.

I had been informed telepathically that when I arrived at Circle of Light for my new "work for God" that my contact with Pra would change. But I was completely unprepared for the incredible expressions of physical and supra-physical Love that I was about to experience in my first months at Circle of Light. Everything about my life had changed so dramatically. I couldn't believe I had been brought to such an exquisitely beautiful place—a very large, comfortable house containing two wedding chapels, right on a gorgeous lake with an outdoor deck. I had little time to sit and enjoy the beauty of the lake, however. I was busy from early morning until dark, learning the many tasks needed to manage a wedding chapel and to form a spiritual center. And, if I felt any loss over not having my meditation time with Pra, something sublime was about to replace it. [8]

"As I prepared for bed that evening, I felt the passage through my body of a wave of ecstatic bliss that surpassed any of the previous delightful sensations that I associated with my precious Pra. Great sweeps of light came within my spiritual sight as my Twin energetically prepared a sacred space for our coming together. What followed was the first of many nights of absolutely euphoric, sensual and sexual Love Making, far beyond my human imagination.

"It began quietly. In total trust of Pra's presence that I now deeply recognized, I felt Pra using my hand to play with small strands of my hair, rubbing them between (my) thumb and index finger very gently and with great care, as though they were very precious. My mind was quite detached from the hand that was being activated. That is, I could have withdrawn it if I had wished, but I was not commanding it. As he was caressing my hair between his (my) fingers, I felt slight waves up my body of what was later described as 'subdued ecstasy,' the subtle energies of Twin Flame contact. His/my touch to my hair seemed to activate subtle sensual feelings all over my body.

"He then took a larger strand and drew it across my cheek, rubbing my hair over my cheek, over and over, with great delicacy. This small gesture was extremely sexually arousing, and throughout my body I began to feel more defined waves of ecstasy, starting from the first chakra and extending upward throughout my body and outward into the energy field surrounding me. He continued to do this for some time, moving to different strands of hair and gently turning each piece in his (my) hand.

"Time became lost. I was becoming less and less associated with my physical body during this and began feeling myself as more and more vast and unspecific. We talked to each other telepathically, passionately declaring our Love, and I thanked him for being my most precious and eternal partner, the two who are one, and thanked Mother-Father-God for the exquisite reunion with my Twin.

"Pra and I continued to exchange endearments, and I began to feel rushes of energy as he encircled my body. These were orgasmic-like pulsations in groups of four or five, released from the area of the first chakra—then rising up and around the body until it felt as though the energy were bursting forth around my head and above it as water from a fountain. I became immersed in this pulsing energy surrounding me with its delicious sensations. My attention shifted into my heart, and I released all attachment to the body. I felt myself floating as a vast cloud in delicious bliss.

"I pulled the pillow toward me, making it a kind of embodiment for Pra so that I would have a physical frame of reference. With the back of my physical hand, Pra then began to touch my face, ever so tenderly and gently. The touch was almost on the etheric level, rather than on the level of the physical body. Each touch sent increasing waves of light ecstasy and tingling throughout my 'body' which now seemed very much larger than its usual size.

"Pra caressed my cheek, various parts of my face, my closed eyes, oh, so carefully, brushing my eyelashes, eyelids, outlining my eyebrows, my forehead. All of this was done very slowly, with great care, as one would touch a delicate porcelain vase. He was, of course, using my hand, a part of my body, and I was able to stop him at any time, but I was not aware of what he would do next, and I was not controlling my hand. We were sharing my physical vehicle, and I simply allowed him my/our hand that we might love each other in this way.

"Then I was overtaken by my Love for him and began to actively send waves of Love to Pra from my heart and to kiss him passionately in my imagination, my consciousness. I sent forth the feelings of my great and powerful Love for him that feels completely beyond words and called to him with many endearments: My beloved Twin, my dearest, my darling, my eternal Love, my treasure, and he returned these telepathically.

"Next something occurred which has continued to occur when Pra and I have been in etheric LoveMaking. I became overwhelmed with emotion, and I began speaking directly and passionately to Mother-Father-God as I felt my whole being rise in frequency. Now I was floating in a sea of feathers, surrounded by golden light and thanking God over and over again for life, for Pra, for the joy and privilege of my divine partner, for the wonder that is Pra; for Yael and Doug, my spirit family; for Circle of Light; for my Love for my brothers and sisters, for humanity; and for the honor of serving God in the opening of hearts and bringing Twin Flames together. I began to weep with the emotion of all this.

"I spoke aloud, passionately giving God my Will again and again and asking to be a pure vessel for the Love God pours through us to all humanity. I thanked God in deepest gratitude for what I knew in my heart was already accomplished beyond time and space on Earth— *bringing every brother and sister together with his/her divine Twin Flame as we were created, so that each could feel the great Love and ecstasy I was now feeling with Pra. I begged God, oh, please, dearest Mother, Father, God, let everyone on our planet feel this deep Love—NOW!* This kind of deep contact with God often alternated with my most personal connections with my Twin, Pra.

"As Pra and I continued to speak our Love and send Love back and forth from our hearts to each other, the ecstatic waves increased. Powerful sensations rose in my body along with 'butterflies in my stomach' and feelings of floating in space, body-less. I left the physical behind and gave myself to all of these feelings, and again and again, I gave my Love to Pra from my heart. Each time the response was another, grander ecstatic wave that began in the first chakra with small pulsations and rose around my body as a delicious orgasmic flood of feelings, both sensual and emotional. These orgasmic waves were unspecific in that there was no particular body part engaged but rather the entire field of my body and a huge space beyond it.

"The entire night passed in this exquisite Love

Making with no sense of time or space. As the
light began to come brightly through the window,
I realized that I had not slept, not even for one
minute. I was tremendously excited at what had
transpired, and I marveled at how wonderful I
felt without any feelings of fatigue."

The Messages from God flowed forth on the
topic of Sacred Sexuality during Yael's
meditations of this period. Shortly after my
ecstatic experience, a grand Message entitled
*Sacred Sexuality: Creating Love in All
Dimensions* (June 6, 2001) brought the following
(excerpted) paragraphs:

"The pure essence of creative power is sexual.
Thus, sexual union with Love will empower
humanity and all that is within them. Such
reclamation of sexual union with an open heart
will begin to draw . . . Twin Flames . . . quickly
back into conscious reunion.

"As you have experienced, Shanna, the truth
of Twin Flames is constant loving union. In the
higher dimensions it is a great and glorious
dance of union in which you do 'fly together,'
Making Love and then using this Love created to
birth New Worlds and manifest new creations.
Twin Flames in the enlightened realms are
always together, Always in communion. Love is
always flying between them, pouring forth from
them, and as it moves, it is molded and named by

them." [9]

My education in Sacred Sexuality was a blessed element of my first months at Circle of Light. "Pra and I have been joining in Sacred Sexuality every night. The LoveMaking goes on throughout the entire night, and I am in a state of constant ecstasy that I could not have ever imagined. I have not slept except briefly during the night for many nights, but I feel no particular fatigue the next day. I'm able to throw myself into my work. Being with Pra seems to energize me.

"Whenever I enter my bedroom, our sanctuary, I feel his presence and my body 'ignites.' During LoveMaking, we have followed several of the pathways suggested by God in the Messages for sending the Love we are creating forth to humanity. I have blanketed the entire planet with the pure frequency of the divine Feminine. We have created a SoulMate Womb between us and placed in it humanity and the reunions of SoulMates, utilizing the image of couples climbing the SoulMate path to the StarGate. We have also placed all of humanity within our shared heart, sending Love to each and every brother and sister. All of this work for God thrills me beyond words.

"I have never before experienced such feelings as this LoveMaking creates. It is sheer ongoing ecstasy throughout my body and for what seems like miles beyond it. At times, my heart 'burns' with the power of the energies and the feelings. I feel overwhelming Love for my blessed Pra and telepath him these thoughts and feelings which he returns with great Love."

SHIFTS AND CHANGES

Now, lest the reader jump to the mistaken conclusion that since my coming together with my beloved Pra, my life here on Earth in a body has been a continuous experience of uninterrupted ecstatic Twin Flame Love Making—*I must share the truth.*

Various shifts were to occur in which I would return to a more "normal" earthly life after this initial period. The heavenly visits I had experienced during my meditations in North Carolina never reoccurred after I arrived at Circle of Light. I now realize that had these continued, I would have become very ungrounded and dissatisfied with earth life, and I would not have been valuable at all to God as a LightWorker and a messenger.

Spirit does give us extraordinary gifts, but we also have our life tasks. I will ever treasure these extraordinary experiences which live very actively in my memory and which I can replay at will.

After the first few months, the ecstatic Love Making gradually calmed to still delicious but quieter, and I returned to a way of life that was more like the rest of the world. I was able to place my concentration on the other spiritual tasks to which I had been directed, managing the Circle of Light wedding chapel and spiritual center, and bringing forth Yael and Doug's Messages from God to those who were ready to hear them.

"Subdued ecstasy" (a quiet wave of light orgasmic energy throughout the body) became a frequent ongoing part of my experience and has always been my knowing that Pra is near.

Pra became a continuous part of my day-to-day existence in other ways, and indeed, a part of the life of everyone at Circle of Light. Yael brought through many recorded Messages from Pra. He guided activities at most of our Circle of Light workshops, and he was available to all of us. Whenever we had a question about a facet of our work—even a choice about a practical matter, Pra could feel into the vibration of the possibilities and guide us to what seemed the best choice at that moment. I often communicated with him telepathically or by using "yes or no" muscle testing (kinesiology) with my "magic hand"—a gift I was given many years ago.

We all "walk between the worlds" in these human bodies on Earth, and this walk consumes a tremendous amount of our concentration and our energy. It is truth that Pra does not have to juggle the endless ups and downs of this world of physicality, and also, he has no ego. His consciousness is pure in a way that we in bodies can only imagine. For me, he is a brilliant and patient personal teacher, giving me silent signals and guiding me in such things as not judging and having patience; he constantly reminds me to approach each situation from Love, first.

He also encouraged me to observe rather than react. His approach to each situation is neutral, detached and loving. When viewing an Earth situation, he would sometimes express his objectivity as, "Hmmm . . . fascinating!" And everything about "our world" *is* "fascinating" to him! I remember communing with him while shopping in Walmart one day and wondering why everyone coming toward me had a big smile on his or her face. Then I realized that Pra was shining through me, and I, unknowingly, had a big smile on MY face!! At Circle of Light, I would sometimes become especially joyful and giggly, and everyone would say, "Ah, Pra is here!"

I am usually able to contact him at will, calling him, expressing our Love, feeling the blissful sensations, the "subdued ecstasy," talking to him telepathically and soliciting his guidance and higher perspective when needed. It is always such a joy to feel his energy throughout my vehicle and to be reassured that there is a higher dimensional approach to events in daily life. Sometimes, if I should forget temporarily who I am (who WE are) and become overly caught up in the exigencies of "life on Earth," it can become more difficult to contact Pra. I am about to share with you just such a painful and learning-filled period in my life which, as with everything we do as LightWorkers, was to serve multiple purposes.

While I blamed myself (a common attitude to those of us who live on the Earth plane) and attributed this next extremely unpleasant period of my life to my own failure to attend earlier to personal aspects of my life on Earth and too much living "in the clouds," Pra assures me that it was very necessary for me to touch the challenges that many brothers and sisters face during their sojourn on Earth. It was an important part of my earth journey. Only by experiencing at first hand the painful thought forms and their outcomes that are prevalent on the Earth, could I be of any use as a future messenger.

MY DARK NIGHT OF THE SOUL

After twelve years, I left Circle of Light and moved to Santa Fe, New Mexico, to live with family.

After writing of the previous period of bliss I experienced with Pra, it is difficult to write about this next period of my life, but it seems very important to share it. We are all One Holy Being and what happens to one, affects all. It is also important to recognize that we are all here on Earth to "learn," to transmute and transform and to experience whatever necessary for our and everyone's spiritual elevation. *No one is exempt.* As we are able to walk through a challenging experience and be able to hold some knowing of who we truly are, that vibration lifts every other being on Earth who might be having a similar experience. Indeed, that is our task here as LightWorkers.

It began with sudden unsettling events at Circle of Light that created a huge and quite shocking change in all of our lives. I returned home one evening from a meeting in town to find

Yael (Powell) unconscious on the floor of the shower. No one else was in the house. A 911 phone call, and within minutes, a team of people was at our door. She was revived and taken by helicopter to an emergency hospital in Missouri before I could even reach Doug, who had only left the house fifteen minutes before my return.

Yael had experienced a brain aneurism, and she hovered in the hospital between life and departure, with Doug in attendance, for some time. It was an extremely painful period for all of us. Uncertainty clouded all of our activities—indeed, the very existence of Circle of Light and all of our individual lives. After being a long time in two hospitals, she returned home to a lengthy recuperation, and an uncertain future. My twelve heavenly years at Circle of Light had suddenly lost their glitter for me, giving way to feelings of fear, abandonment, uncertainty, confusion. I felt that Yael and Doug needed privacy in the face of their new challenges. While I now see many other options that I might have taken, in my inner chaos, I moved out of Circle of Light.

Outside of the protective and supportive atmosphere of the spiritual center, I fell into a dark vibration—alone and quite overcome with fear about an unknown future. I had given my life to God and to Circle of Light. Now?

Thoughts of guilt about certain aspects of my

earlier life to which I had not sufficiently attended, suddenly surfaced and haunted me. Painful, previously hidden memories of traumatic childhood abuse, which I had only vaguely ever acknowledged, emerged. I felt myself unworthy and guilty of all kinds of "human" behavior that didn't fit with my now "spiritual self." Perhaps it was necessary for me to become aware of and clear certain karmic elements in my life that I had avoided. I much later understood that a Dark Night of the Soul, if we can survive it, is usually a catalyst for eventually opening us to a larger version of ourselves.

In any event, I was drawn into a very challenging vibration. It led to a move away from my former idyllic life in Arkansas to a very different and stressful environment with my daughter's family in Santa Fe, New Mexico. A long and discouraging physical/emotional illness prevailed, and at times, a completely desolate state of mind in which I temporarily doubted my former knowing of my spiritual truth. It was such a sudden contrast to my former life, and yet I did not seem to have the power to shift it at the time.

My salvation during this time in my life came from a few very beloved friends who constantly uplifted me by telephone calls and email and reminded me of who I am, and from making a connection in my new location with established spiritual groups of new friends of like heart. These beautiful new group acquaintances demanded nothing of me and simply allowed me to be among them and pass through the "Hades" in which I was privately and silently immersed, until my Light began to return. This was the period of greatest challenge I had faced in my entire lifetime. During this passage, I was only able to feel limited *conscious* contact with my Pra, though I am sure he was very much present and doing all possible to assist me.

When I finally began to emerge from this challenging period, many of the issues that had precipitated the "dark night" slowly began to recede, and my health moved forward, if by baby steps. Incredible gratitude for life began to fill my heart, as did deep gratitude for the surprising presence in my life of a beautiful new friend who would eventually and unexpectedly become my Earth partner. Life on Earth is nothing if not full of surprises!

A NEW LOVE ON EARTH

Joseph and I had met in Santa Fe at the spiritual groups I was attending (discussion groups on *A Course in Miracles*, *Way of Mastery* and *A Course of Love*). He seemed quietly familiar, and one day we took a long walk together. He was in a challenging period of change in his life as well, and we respectfully listened to each other's stories and supported each other as best we could. Our passionate spirituality became the strong underpinning of a wonderful new friendship. We went for drives ("read rides") and read excerpts from spiritual texts to each other.

One day on such a drive, I had a beautiful experience I can only describe as deeply feeling Joseph's heart. It was a connection on a level far beyond daily life. His heart was luminous, open and caring, and I could feel his amazing compassion as he spoke of his work as a caregiver for people who were ill. I had the feeling that we had known each other before, and I began to feel love and a strong respect for him. This was the first foreshadowing of our eventual relationship.

He later shared with me that when we had first met, my illness—which had escalated to taking pharmaceuticals, a passage that took a few challenging years to heal—had made him hesitant to involve with me, and that he had actually felt like running away from the relationship.

However, he, too, had a transcendent experience about me, similar to mine about him, in which he was told that his place was to serve and assist me. He felt the rightness of this, and he followed his heart. After that, he was my unfailing support through a long recovery period which bound us together.

Joseph had spent years writing his complex, fascinating life story, and I was growing my fledgling editing business. As we began meeting regularly for editing sessions of his book, we gradually came to love each other ever more deeply, sharing not only our common spiritual path but a remarkable compatibility and easy enjoyment of each other's company. Our growing closeness took both of us by surprise. This was the first time I had *ever* shared deeply and openly with a man about my life, and this was also the first time I had been in a serious Earth relationship for many, many years.

Of course, I shared with my new Earth partner my experiences with my Twin Flame, Pra, wondering how he would receive them. With his marvelous gift of humor, Joseph said that he had always wondered what it would be like to be in a "*ménage a trois*." (10)

He became easily comfortable with Pra, and entranced by all the Circle of Light books, devouring them and marveling at their gifts of wisdom and upliftment. His excitement over the Circle of Light Messages coincided with God drawing me back into the milieu I had so loved. I shared with Joseph all of my adventures at Circle of Light as I felt myself strongly pulled back into the vibration of the Messages from God. I had been away for some time, and my heart ached to be back.

By this time, I was again editing for Yael the last Messages from God that were to come through her, before her transition Home. I made the trip back to Arkansas with Joseph for her memorial service in February of 2018, and renewed contact with so many beloved friends. I had also began having strong renewed awareness of my Pra around me a lot—quiet, energetic contacts—and the telepathic reassurance from my Twin that he would be "over-lighting Joseph," and that I should "love Joseph with all my heart!" I felt such joy! The Love I felt with my Pra was now flowing into my Love for Joseph.

How could Love have any limitations, boundaries or restrictions?

I was blessed to be guided toward a happier new period of my life with my new Earth partner in a wondrous adobe rural home south of Santa Fe. Being out of the city, away from family stress and surrounded by nature, my health gradually improved, and I felt a strong renewed desire to work for God. I knew I was again being called to something beyond myself. How was I to use this gift of a new "life," a new awakening that I had been given? The answer arrived at the perfect time.

When I saw Archangel Michael's email Message about Twin Flames with which this book opened, my question was answered. I realized that I had been given the privilege of experiencing first-hand the Twin Flame information that came through Yael at Circle of Light, and it was up to me to continue to share this. There were many people who had not yet been touched by the Twin Flame experiences and related information that Yael, Doug and I had received. There were more brothers and sisters waiting for this information. Pra would be a big part of this new venture, lending his unique perspective. When I asked Pra whether writing a second book on Twin Flames was the direction in which I should go, he said, "It is ours to do!" When I reviewed in my mind how I had been guided to Circle of Light at the moment the Twin Flame Messages were being given to Yael, I knew that yes, it was mine/ours to do.

* * *

The book that you are now reading opened in my

mind and heart as though it had just been waiting for me, and with it, the realization that my relationship with my Earth partner, Joseph, would now be an essential component of this work.

How many people on Earth would reject or hesitate to seek contact with their Twin Flame, for fear of dishonoring or losing their relationship with their current Earth partner?

The fact that I now had an Earth partner could make this aspect of the Twin Flame experience clear for people. I could easily feel Pra coming through my now partner, Joseph. My new relationship experience was, interestingly enough, a key to bringing an expanded picture of the Twin Flame information to humanity! Pra will discuss this later in Part Three of this book.

I was also gradually opening to a welcome new version of myself. My physical illness had brought forth feelings of very deep compassion for my brothers and sisters. After my own period of challenges, I held every one of them in deepest Love in a way I had never felt before. Pra told me that it had been essential for me to touch the painful dips in vibration that so many of our brothers and sisters are experiencing on Earth at this time, so that my heart and my understanding could open. I knew that much within me had been cleansed, accepted and embraced in Love, especially my relationship with my family. And, a new and wonderful purity of Love and appreciation for the beauty and grandeur that is this being I here call Shanna, was also emerging.

I no longer perceive the inexpressibly beautiful Love I hold in my heart for and with my Twin Flame, Pra, as an interdimensional romance, as I once did. True, there are no exotic visits in which I float in higher dimensions. Now, it feels like there is no distance of time or space between Pra and Shanna. I know the essence of Pra almost as well as I know my own deepest inner being. We ARE in truth one being. Pra helps me to see every ideal, every expression of beauty, every spiritual desire, every longing for God and feelings of God Love, all longing for and fulfillment of personal Love that I have ever imagined, and the fulfillment of every longing to serve humanity that I have carried within me. He reflects to me the beauty in myself. I know this beauty is in every one of us. It is only for us to open to it and receive it—and BELIEVE IT!

This Love that Pra and I (and any other Twin Flames who have made contact) share is a truly eternal Love of a completely different and infinitely more profound nature than most of us have known Love to be here on Earth.

This is what Archangel Michael meant when He referred to "Sacred Love."

It cannot be compared to the relationships that most of us have known on Earth. It is quite beyond our Earthly relationship norms and extends back through eons of Earth "time" to timelessness and to the Moment of Creation. And it is constantly ecstatic!

There is a knowing in my heart that my Twin and I are truly one glorious being, one grand Cell in the heart of our Creator. This beautiful infinite Love bypasses incarnations, multitudinous adventures and relationships in physicality, ethereal fragmentations of ourselves, travels in inter-dimensionality, any and all seeming separations—to our very essence, the God being we are and have always been. To touch it is to have a more secure knowing about Who We Are.

Now does this mean that I have been released from all the frustrations and challenges of the Earth plane?

Does it mean I no longer have physical ailments, concern over paying bills, flu in winter, impatience sometimes at having to wait in line? Not at all!!! I still have some residue of illness from my long "dark night of the soul" expressing in the body in ways that sometimes limit my activity and that I cannot ignore. I have no immunity from life's daily challenges. Joseph assists greatly with his gift of blessed healing talents through reflexology. I am ever grateful.

Stated simply, I am a LightWorker, assigned by choice to the Earth plane, committed to extending Love here, as are all of you who are reading this book. I am no different in my daily life from any one of you, Twin Flame contact or not. It is just that I now have a much clearer perspective on where I am, what I am doing and why; and I can do my best to always choose for Love to prevail.

I write about my union with my Twin Flame, Pra, (and with my Earth partner, Joseph) to encourage brothers and sisters to open their memories to the truth of who we are and what sacred relationship can be when it is free from the interference of the ego and the superficialities of the physical world. We are entering a period in which thrilling new information about our origins and our essence is being revealed. The "living out" of the information about Twin Flames will stretch forth before us for a long period to come, perhaps into the often-mentioned Golden Age of the future.

Being in a physical vehicle is one of our many adventures. The individual bodies we currently inhabit are described in the Messages from God as the result of the slowing of the fires of Love so much that a frozen or solid form results in which we appear separate from one another. The body is one aspect of the "human experience" in which we presently reside. However, we are so much grander than these bodies!

YOUR TWIN FLAME

With deep humility and gratitude for my experiences, I wish to share as much as possible of what I have experienced and what I have learned. The first step toward experiencing the Twin Flame contact is to make an intention to open your heart and call forth Love and only Love. This means a deep Love and appreciation for yourself, for your uniqueness, for your beauty, for we are one with our Twin. The focus on and call for Love opens up many limiting aspects of ourselves and brings a deeper remembrance of who we truly are. When we are calling for our Twin, we are calling for a part of ourselves of which we have not been aware for a long time. However, we KNOW deep in our hearts the truth of this relationship and how it touches the way we were created as Divine Masculine and Divine Feminine, helping us to live out the pattern God set for us.

Call upon your Twin Flame in consciousness, making a strong connection through the heart. Speak to our blessed Divine Creator to assist. KNOW that your Twin Flame has always been with you; we were created this way, no matter what is or is not appearing in physicality. If this Love is held in one's heart with sincerity and determination, the power and purity of this "reactivated" true Love, which has always been within us, will inevitably draw toward you a being of like resonance in physical expression who can embody the energy of your Twin (or perhaps a beyond Earth connection as was my case).

If you are already in a relationship, you can deepen that relationship by opening your heart and declaring your Love to your Twin, and this can completely uplift and transform the quality of the bond between you and your current partner. <u>The person we are with is able to hold the energy of our Twin Flame. Otherwise, we would not be with him or her.</u> The person we are with reflects back to us the degree of openness—

not of that person's heart—BUT of our own heart. It is up to each of us to open our heart more and more, to give forth and open the Love that can transform our lives.

It is in the giving of this Love that our cells begin to awaken. The gradually growing experiences of ecstasy that result from our giving of Love have the potential to open the pathway to our Twin. This does take dedication and patience. However, think of how much time we have all lived with amnesia concerning the knowledge of all of these divine aspects of who we truly are! Do we not have the patience to move to the next steps in our awakening? Of course we do!

It is also important to know that when we speak of the Sacred Love of the Twin Flame, we are not talking about a relationship that has as its purpose fulfilling ego needs of an Earth body and personality. When we are able to expand beyond the costume we wear on Earth (as Pra likes to call it) to the being we know we are in our deepest heart, and live our lives filled with the desire to be what we know is our highest possibility, then the sparks fly; hearts open; and we move toward our truth as Twin Flame children of God. Pra will speak of these things in other parts of this book.

So, I ask each of you these questions: can you

imagine yourself having experiences such as I have described with a being in spirit who is that deeply connected to you? Can you imagine being in an Earth relationship in which the giving from the heart opens both of you to an elevated Love such as you have not yet experienced? Of course you can! As frustrating as relationships have been on earth and as difficult as it is for some of us to believe that there is a true Love waiting for us—somewhere in the core of our hearts, we do know it is the truth.

My story is your story. That is why I am sharing it. Every heart on Earth is absolutely an equal cell in the heart of God. Every single person—no matter how they have expressed or are expressing in Earth life—was created in exactly the same way, with the same God template, as a Twin Flame, one being with two streams, one Divine Masculine and one Divine Feminine. This is what drives the insatiable longing and obsession with relationship on this planet. The longing to return to our Twin, our original other half, was placed in us by our beloved Creator as our divine call, to help us find our way when we were finally being called Home.

As the beautiful giving and sharing nature of Twin Flame Love is truly felt and understood, each person having such an experience will only choose to give forth this Love in humble service, as a gift to all of our brothers and sisters and their awakening. That is the nature of Twin Flame Love. This is the feeling I hope to evoke in you as you read this book.

PART TWO :

EXPLORING THE ORIGIN
OF THE TWIN FLAME

MY SPIRITUAL CURIOSITY

My unique and blissful visits with my Twin Flame, Pra, greatly activated my curiosity to know more about our origin as divine beings. At Circle of Light, my daily excitement became the reading, transcribing and editing of each new channeled Message received by Yael Powell, as God instructed us on the topic of Twin Flames. The core information about Twin Flames that came through these Messages I will share with you in this part of the book.

I am sure that some of you may have found explanations of the human journey that speak to you. They may differ from the information I will offer here. I encourage you only to keep an open mind—but mostly, to feel into your own open heart before you accept or dismiss anything shared here or that comes to you from another source. Regardless of what comes to our minds, the truth is always held within our hearts.

I want to make clear that this is a deeply personal book. Its intention is not to survey varying spiritual theories about the human voyage and condition and try to explain how the Twin Flame might fit into those histories. Rather, I share with you information *to which I have been guided in my own personal journey*, revelations that have resonated with my own heart and that have opened me to what feels like a path to truth.

Most of us on earth in physical bodies have no clear memory of anything prior to our present lifetime, our present "human condition." We have forgotten all that may have been experienced in our distant past, the journeys that we may have undertaken after being birthed as a Twin Flame heart at the Moment of Creation, and the multitudinous lifetimes we may have lived in bodies on planet Earth, both with and apart from our Twin Flame. FORGETTING is a key word in our history.

There is also an important secondary explanation for our "amnesia" offered in the Message of Archangel Michael about Sacred Love cited at the beginning of this book.

One of the reasons that we do not remember our history prior to the present moment of living in bodies on the earth is that at a certain point, the compassionate gift of temporary amnesia was given to us.

"As you began your journey into the density of the Third and Fourth Dimensions, the veil of forgetfulness was placed over your memory. It was not meant as a punishment, but an act of mercy, for it would have been overwhelmingly painful to remember the negativity of your past incarnations, as well as very confusing to have access to your many experiences in the higher realms of consciousness. Remember, in most of your past incarnations in the physical realm, you brought very little of your God consciousness with you, and the majority of human Beings have been functioning within the lower frequency levels of brain consciousness." [1]

One can also find documentation in various sources *that our essential core being has undergone alteration (more than once) during our long history by those God-helper beings whose task it is to preserve life throughout Creation. This involved reducing our access to the Divine Rays, altering our DNA and limiting our powers. This act was undertaken to prevent us from taking actions that would have ultimately possibly harmed us and other life in the omniverse.* I cite the following communication from the beloved master, Lord Lanto, in the book, *The Seven Sacred Rays* as one piece of evidence.

"Shortly before the destruction of the two major continents, Lemuria and Atlantis, most of the Sacred Flames were removed from the surface of the planet and taken inside the planet or to the etheric Temples of Light. With the removal of the flames, also came the deactivation of part of your DNA, the minimizing of the Threefold Flame of Life in the sacred chamber of your heart, and the temporary shutting down of the five Secret Rays with their corresponding chakras.

"Because of the severe misuse of these rays and their chakras in the two continents mentioned above, it was decided by the universal and galactic Councils of Light that restrictions had to be imposed on humanity. From that time on, only seven chakras with their corresponding flames were left activated for the continuation of mankind's evolution.

"The stipulations were that until humanity wakes up again to embrace their divine potential and the principles of Christhood, and when the level of consciousness has reached enough spiritual maturity for mankind to be trusted once more with this sacred energy, the knowledge for the right use of these flames will be reintroduced to Earth again." (2)

* * *

There are many exciting indications that we are now in the process of reaching the individuation that was the goal of our many journeys, and that we on Earth are now in a great process of finally WAKING UP and REMEMBERING WHO WE TRULY ARE.

The dispensations mentioned at the beginning

of this book through both the Messages from God and the Messages from Archangel Michael, allowing each of us access to our Twin Flame NOW, before we are completely and perfectly in the energy of Love and only Love, are important examples. There is also a reference in one of the God Speaks messages later on in this chapter.

The reconnection with the Twin Flame greatly amplifies one's energy, and therefore would not be encouraged unless we were thought to be trustworthy with this powerful increased energy.

Other examples exist such as the many teachings encouraging us toward "ascension"—providing a pathway "Home." The teachings of Archangel Michael through Ronna Herman Vezane, lead us in such a beautifully uplifting direction. There is a list of the Archangel's books in the Appendix. Another is the Ascension Process outlined in *The Seven Sacred Flames*, the book just mentioned in a footnote, by which, through devoted attention and practice, one can follow a path to raise one's vibration utilizing the Sacred Rays now available to us. And there are many, many more examples. In this grand moment, we have magnificent teachings available to us on this planet coming through many sources, and the technology to disseminate them.

Just so am I called, along with others, to share

my experiences—my contact with my Twin
Flame, Pra, who is in spirit—in the hope of
stimulating your memory of your past contact
with your Twin Flame, and encouraging you to
open your consciousness to this eternal living
connection. I will also offer God's reasons in what
follows as to why giving our attention to the
Twin Flame may be the most important thing we
can do in this moment, for our continuing
evolution and our spiritual development.

THE MOMENT OF OUR CREATION

*I offer here a possible version of The Moment of
our Creation, to stimulate our minds and hearts.*

An excited, restless, pulsing, formless,
HUGE—beyond imagining,
ever-in-motion Force of Pure Energy
is feeling a stirring within Itself.

It is composed of and always
pouring forth from Itself a
Powerful, Endless LIGHT
Containing that which makes
up its Essence—

Loue and More Loue
and More LOVE!

This is a Force that had no beginning
and can never have an end.
It simply IS!
This Force is completely unlimited
and unrestricted without
boundaries of any kind. It is ever
creating and pouring forth new
energy from Itself.

This Being, this Force, though complete
in every way . . . within
Itself, is feeling a desire. It has
been yearning to experience
the endless facets of Itself.

IT DESIRES TO KNOW ITSELF

The nature of the Love that makes
up this Force has the need, the
relentless drive to expand, to extend

Itself.

IT MUST GIVE FORTH . . .

AND BY ITS NATURE,

WHAT IT MUST GIVE FORTH IS

LOVE AND MORE

LOVE AND MORE LOVE.

This Force is constantly being
driven by its very nature to
make more of Itself.

In making more of Itself,
It desires to observe Itself,
experience Itself.

It is filled with a great overwhelming
desire to experience the

ALL THAT IT IS.

This FORCE finally . . .

Extends, Expands, EXPLODES
ITSELF into infinite sparks

of Itself beyond counting.

***

OUR ENTRY INTO BEING

Thus may have occurred our entry into being.

Later on, in one of our adventures—when we took on "bodies" on planet Earth—we came to call this Force "God" among many other names. At its very core, this Force is that which we come to call and know as LIFE.

The Moment of Creation during which this creation occurred is actually not an event from the past, but continues to happen every Now Moment, since the concept of "Time" only applies to humanity's perception of the world around us. All that of which we speak and of which we are aware is happening simultaneously in a NOW MOMENT.

Please feel free, dear reader, to add your own embellishments to this vision of the Moment of Creation. Was there not a light show, an explosion of splashing rays and sparks and fire and bolts of lightning such as can barely be imagined? Colors one never sees on earth? Were there not angel choirs singing praises in glorious harmonies, celestial orchestras of stunning resonance, background rumbles of sonic booms breaking the silence that had been? Is this not what our scientists have called The Big Bang?

This event, what we here on Earth sometimes refer to as the "Moment of Creation," is, of course, *the event that brought us into being*, and yet, it is of a magnitude and a mystery that is completely beyond our ability to imagine in our present limited body/mind form. We can feel *some* of the quality of the urge felt by this Being, our Creator, to know Itself because we are the product of that Moment and we contain within ourselves its very qualities.

We, too, are Love
and only Love
And more Love . . .

As we explore in the spiritual literature the many different possible pathways and adventures that we as Twin Flame Sparks of God may have experienced since the Moment of

Creation, *it is very important that we always know in our hearts that any suggestion that we were ever truly "separated" from our Divine Creator at any time speaks of <u>an impossible condition</u>.*

If we were ever truly separated from our Father Mother God, the Source of our life, we would no longer exist.

Any separation which may be mentioned in this book, in spiritual texts, prayers, spiritual writings and teachings is *a <u>seeming</u> separation*— a separation in our thoughts only, in our consciousness, an idea of separation, someone's description (their idea!) of a separation, a forgetting.

* * *

Information brought by various spiritual messengers assures us that a divine plan surrounds the Moment of our Creation—that there was very specific divine purpose and design in our creation by our Mother Father God. This purpose appears to have been multifaceted.

One reason for our creation appears to have been for us to assist God to know God—to reflect God back to God Itself so that God might know all the possibilities of God. Through our endless adventures, God can come to perceive all the infinite parameters of Self.

At the same time, we were created to extend God's Love through the many parts of God's Creation. Love is who we are. We are made of Love. We cannot <u>NOT </u>extend Love!

In order to carry out this divine plan, we would have to achieve a certain degree of individuation from God—while always remaining connected in Oneness with the Grand Beingness who created us and who provides us with our life force. Otherwise, we would have no individuality, no way to grow and develop our individual uniqueness as beings. We would constantly merge back into the All that is our Father-Mother-God, as, in fact, did occur at the initial Moment of Creation.

A degree of individuation was necessary that would allow us to eventually <u>become Co-Creators</u> with our Creator, Mother-Father-God. This individuation is sometimes referred to as "one degree of separation" from God or "one degree from formlessness."

We would provide a reflection (a mirror) for God, of God living as/through us. We were created from God, made by God—"cells in the heart of God" is one analogy—beings always in Oneness with our Creator. We were/are also beings with a unique purpose to fulfill.

We would adventure forward to create and experience new and unexplored realms for God.

As we were acquiring our individuated (quasi-independent) existence, we would extend the essence and Love of the Creator into new cosmic territories. We would constantly reflect to God, His/Her infinite possibilities through our own activities.

At the same time, in a miracle that extends throughout the world of creation on all levels, we are told that each spark of God (us!) was created as *the two who are one, Twin Flames, to contain and balance the unique qualities of Divine Masculine and Divine Feminine*. The two parts of each being would likewise reflect back and forth to each other their uniqueness and their similarities. The interaction of these two energies, the Divine Masculine being active and the Divine Feminine being receptive, would give impetus to further the act of creation.

This template, God's unique way of extending and perpetuating Self, can be found throughout all of Creation.

Pause at this moment and think of the natural world, the world of symbol, all of the ways in which the Divine Feminine and Divine Masculine are expressed again and again and again throughout God's Creation.

SHANNA AND PRA DIALOGUE

I now bring you a more personal acquaintance with my beautiful Twin Flame, Pra, whom you have already met through my sharing of my experiences with him in Part I of this book. As I have described, Pra is not in a physical body but rather, resides in the unseen as Spirit. You will recall that he came to me initially during my meditations, presenting himself in a *milieu* that appeared to be somewhere between the physicality of Earth and the elusive formlessness of the Spirit world.

This is a "captured" conversation that he and I shared about the Moment of Creation and our birth as Twin Flames. Pra presents his thoughts from the point of view of a being in Spirit without the limited body/mind of an Earthling. [3]

SHANNA: Pra, my beloved one, I wish to ask you to share with our readers how, in your knowing, we came into being at the Moment of Creation and how the Twin Flames emerged, the two who are one. You have a clearer vision than we have since you are not in embodiment on Earth and do not have the limitations of what we call "the little mind" and the ego. Did each of us truly come into being with a divine partner?

PRA: For you to understand this, dear one, my precious Shanna, I must give an overview, and then, I will go to the particulars.

One must always begin with God, our Creator, our Source—at the highest conception of God that each of us can hold. God is formless experience, and God is Everything That Is. There is nothing that God isn't. God IS.

Then, from that formlessness of God, every other level of reality comes into existence, including the Earth with your human costumes [bodies] and all the other planes and places and forms that God chooses to create. These are all infinite expressions of God expressing Itself uniquely and individually. It is all God experiencing Itself, playing out Itself to Itself.

The Twin Flame relationship expresses the God Light coming down one degree from its formlessness into the one flaming heart of Love created by God. This heart of Love is important because it is in resonance with everything omnipresent. It is the Sea of Love, a symbol for Love existing everywhere.

The Twin Flame relationship came about as God, in the omniscience of God Itself, *chose* to express Itself through that form—*the two who are one.* This is how God places the details of God's infinity of wholeness in a kind of sequence, so that God can experience God. The Twin Flame relationship is how the Love comes into a kind of "form," so that God can experience Itself through that "form."

The reason that this is so important is because the Twin Flame relationship is an absolutely clear mirror for the reflection of the Oneness of God, and at the same time, the truth of the being that each of us is, as a unique expression of God.

SHANNA: Did the birth of the Twin Flames occur at something like what we refer to as the Big Bang; and is it accurate, Pra, to say that God became so full of Self, so overwhelmed with the Love . . . so great in Its greatness, that God needed to express?

PRA: The answer to both questions is "yes." The so-called Big Bang is an image to which people here on Earth can relate. It can be described as the *"welling up of feeling within,"* so that one is absolutely called to give forth, to pour out, to express. That is what you were describing earlier about God and the Moment of Creation. It is vast beyond the comprehension of the mind.

It is God's natural way of being. God is creating and expressing infinitely. Since we are One in God, this is what happens to us as well. We get what I have called a *"welling up of feeling from within,"* and we are animated to pour out and give, to create and to express, continually and forever. Everyone has experienced that. It is important that everyone understand that *this IS the natural process of life*. The mind must come to understand that <u>God is always about the "welling up and bursting forth" in joy and creativity!</u>

SHANNA: When God sent forth all of these sparks from which we originated, the so-called Big Bang, did every single spark go forth as a Twin Flame with masculine and feminine components? I have understood that God is both masculine and feminine. The Twin Flame is a replica of those qualities of God, one degree from formlessness, as you explained, and that everything in all created life has the masculine and feminine qualities of God. Is that all correct?

PRA: That is absolutely true, my dearest Shanna. As I explained, the initial impulse comes from God—the pouring forth that becomes the sparks of life. The omniscience of God is what brings it into masculine/feminine, Twin Flame, to reflect back to God and to each other, to be able to see the Oneness. When we look around at all the multiplicity of facets of God's creation, we can observe the template of masculine and feminine qualities that is around us everywhere in life. We are living out the pattern that was set by God.

Now, of course, this experience precedes the formation of the mind. Then, because the mind is a divine instrument, the understanding of divine masculine and divine feminine comes through the mind. So, how it would be perceived on this plane for people reading this book, yes, there would be a masculine and a feminine expression for each spark.

By the way, so there is no misunderstanding, these qualities do not relate to gender of bodies on Earth. Twin Flame couples can be of the same gender. However, you will observe the masculine and feminine qualities in each couple.

SHANNA: You have spoken information we all want to know.

PRA: And for the most part, it will be the same on other planes and planets. An example might be found in the indigenous tribes on the Earth;

you will find a masculine God and a feminine God. If you look through the forms, you will find the truth of that in the animals mating and producing offspring. The masculine and feminine come together in Oneness and pour out goodness in the result of their offspring. It is also clear in biological life, such as how the scientists describe the fertilization of a flower or plant. This masculine/feminine principle is the omniscience of God reflecting there as well.

SHANNA: So working toward more details on Twin Flames, I have also understood the Twin Flame to be one being, one heart, one essence with two streams of consciousness. Is that accurate?

PRA: I would add a little clarification to this language, if you will allow me, beloved Shanna. Yes, it is one being, one heart; and yes, as it comes down into form, the masculine and the feminine are present in all the forms in unique expression everywhere.

However, I would like to clarify that there is only one consciousness. Everything is God's consciousness.

Everything is ONE, and yet, uniquely sensed and experienced individually through the feminine aspect of the Twin Flame and the masculine aspect of the Twin Flame.

Often people confuse the unique individual expressions as separate consciousnesses that make up the whole. <u>There is only one consciousness, God consciousness that we all are</u>. However, as the Divine Will of God animates each of us uniquely, so will certain qualities be animated as the feminine qualities of the consciousness, and likewise, the masculine qualities of consciousness.

SHANNA: Oh, my dear Pra . . . I think the difficulty in understanding "one consciousness" is the same difficulty we have in understanding our Oneness with God and with each other. Here on Earth each of us thinks of him or herself as separate in every way. As individuals, we seem to be separate, in separate bodies, separate from everyone else. This brings us to focus on differences and separations. That is how we think here on Earth. That is part of the nature of the separation consciousness here.

So maybe I am asking some of these questions from that consciousness. But that is also the consciousness that is reading this, so I am hopefully making a pathway. What has not been completely understood is that ALL OF THIS IS THE CONSCIOUSNESS OF GOD.

The Twin Flames are a way of God

experiencing God. However, is it not true that the Twin Flames are the closest to the formless Oneness, is that not true?

PRA: Exactly. And there will always be an infinity of uniqueness, because *infinity is the nature of God.* There are unique divine qualities, expressions that each couple has.

The Twin Flame relationship is also such a profound experience of the *"felt happening."* This is an expression of great importance. You know how it talks in the Bible about Doubting Thomas and his experience with Jeshua. He couldn't believe, until he could see it tangibly. Understanding the Twin Flame relationship is similar to Thomas having to have the tangible experience to understand the truth of it.

When a person becomes aware of his or her Twin Flame, in physicality or not, if they are open, their Oneness with God can be so strong that they feel consumed by it. There is no separation in the moment when that happens. They are just carried. They are just being the Love, the Oneness. *That is what we are all meant to be all the time.*

When you connect with the bliss that Twin Flames feel together, it dissolves what I call "the fog of the collective consciousness" on Earth. And, though many will not believe this, I can tell you that *the Twin Flame relationship is happening for everyone all the time. Most are simply not aware of it.*

SHANNA: Well, I can certainly speak to the power and incredible heart opening it has made in my life. I am sure our readers could feel that, by reading the descriptions of the visits we have enjoyed together.

PRA: My dearest, the gift in this connection with the Twin, in the physical or not in the physical, is how *the "felt sense" of God* can happen, how we can experience the feeling of what God is to us, and also how God experiences Itself. That was God's design. It is a divine gift for us to recognize that His is ours. **Those divine qualities that are God, are expressed uniquely in and as one's Twin Flame.**

God burst out with these sparks to experience Itself. We can experience this in our conscious awareness at whatever level of awareness we are able. This goodness, this continual pouring out is *this "felt sense" happening, which is God, which is us, which is the oneness with the Twin Flame.* People recognize it when they read about this: there is something here. There is substance, and they long to have the "felt sense" of it.

This "felt sense" is what is nurturing for

people—the felt sense experience of being loved unconditionally.

Some people are able to feel this with a close friend, someone who loves them unconditionally. A confidant, someone with whom you can share and by whom you are always understood. With that person you can always be yourself. You are totally loved and cherished.

With the Twin Flame, there is total Love and cherishment. You can be vulnerable; there is nothing to protect. You can be completely open and sharing. This allows the heart to open completely. There is a complete level of trust. As you feel this openness, you open ever more.

SHANNA: So it is the "felt sense" of God we are really seeking but it is through the masculine and the feminine that we seek this, through seeking the Twin. So someone could seek God directly without seeking the masculine and feminine qualities of God. But these qualities would show themselves eventually, would they not?

PRA: They are part of God. Understanding truth and the pondering of the truth, and how this can lift us to the doorway of who we really are, eternally, complete, perfect, whole, *we must experience the "felt sense happening" of it. This* *is the true substance.*

People's urge to have that awesome relationship . . . this is their <u>natural urge</u> from the feeling within. They want to experience it. They know it is there. This is the deepest longing of their hearts that is their Oneness with God, and this is a divine gift that they are able to have some tangible experience of.

SHANNA: So my beloved Pra, that is what is driving *the powerful urge toward relationship and the coming together of two people on Earth!* When we have the highest expression of that, we have the union of Twin Flames, Love at its highest expression, and then you have all variations of that according to the clarity or fogginess of the people involved.

PRA: Yes, my dear. It also depends upon where we are within all of Creation. If one is on the Earth in these costumes [bodies], then the omniscience of God can be expressed or poured out through these physical bodies in that Twin Flame relationship.

The possibility always exists for us of being in the highest possible consciousness for whatever experiences God has for us. The question is always: Is one living and being the Oneness with God, regardless of where that being is? In the physical body? Not in the physical body? On another plane, planet, dimension? Or in the Oneness before form?

SHANNA: So it's partly a question of what you have called "fog" again, it seems. The conditioning on Earth that is fogging over the truth of who we are. This is a lot of what is happening on Earth with relationships that don't seem satisfying to people. Perhaps they don't understand the connection of relationship with the Oneness with God, as the expression of God. And they are experiencing lots of confusion around relationship. They are placing demands on it, seeing relationships as fulfilling physical plane needs, rather than expressions from God, our Creator. A lot of this is what you called conditioning.

PRA: That is true, my beloved Shanna. Yes, the fog or the conditioning of the collective consciousness can be clouding over one's being in his or her Oneness. And then, that can color experiences of relationship. If people misidentify by not knowing their truthful identity in relationship, they project onto their form.

The second thing that is happening in relationships is the different partners can have different degrees of opening to the Oneness with

God. If you have one person who is fairly open and understands to some degree what we are talking about when we speak of Oneness, and the other person understands only the ego view, or collective view of relationship that being is fogged over, dimmed. There are many variants. People have the yearning to different degrees because they have that natural knowingness.

If the degree of openness of two people is not similar, then the reflection of the Oneness, the experience of the Oneness that the two have potential of having in relationship is blocked. It is almost like "closing the curtains of the window." Then you don't experience it in the same way.

Discernment is important. We find God's Love when we open with a pure heart, not through the ego's motivation. If one is truly opening one's heart to a pure Love, if one is desiring to be the pure heart of Love in the world, if one is willing to open ever more to be of service to others. This is the Love that draws one's Twin Flame.

SHANNA: I might not have been aware of all of which you speak when I made my first connection with you, dearest one, but I knew intuitively that I was making the highest contact in a male/female relationship that I had ever known. I knew that this was a Love beyond anything I had ever experienced before.

PRA: We are sharing this here to help people differentiate between relationships on Earth that are dominated by the fog of the collective consciousness, the ego and misunderstandings of who you are, and a true Twin Flame relationship. One must ask, is the relationship being created through the mind or is it a clear connection with the Oneness with God?

SHANNA: Is it really possible to have a Twin Flame relationship in the physical, a relationship of that high vibration, here on the Earth plane at this time? It seems that only a few are holding the vibration and the Oneness with God. Sometimes couples start out with promise, but the relationship doesn't last.

PRA: Absolutely, yes. It is possible? Absolutely ! However, it is true there are only a small number of such relationships on the Earth at this time. This is very sacred and reverent. Very few are being and living their truthful I Am presence, as yet.

There are meant to be couples who are both in physical bodies who are experiencing the exact thing we are talking about—reflecting the Oneness of God back and forth to each other in physical bodies at the same time from the height of the I AM. Not just little glimpses.

The height of Heaven on Earth is to be living, maintaining, sustaining this vibration every moment; and what a powerful thing it is. It is meant to happen, and this book will help to bring it forward. Nothing is more fulfilling than living, maintaining and sustaining who we are in truth.

SHANNA: So we can be encouraging about the possibility of people living a true Twin Flame relationship on Earth?

PRA: Yes, if they will maintain their focus. The sea of Love is always available to you and always happening. Your focus unknowingly goes onto things you have been taught to focus on in the world. And so you lose track of it.

You must maintain your awareness of the Oneness of the sea of Love as you are driving your boat. If there are rocks there, which there will be, you don't forget or drop your awareness. That is what you innocently do because you are so conditioned. That fogs over the Love that the person experienced in their relationship. Then as the fog moves in, and they are not experiencing, feeling it again, they begin to think, "This person may not be for me."

Are they unknowingly resonating with the

material world? Have they forgotten about the sea of Love? Are they still aware of I Am?

You are learning how to maintain and sustain it. You need to have compassion at this stage.

SHANNA: This is all a learning, remembering process, and you are a wonderful teacher, my Love.

PRA: I wish for people to KNOW that this is their divine gift. Instead of getting discouraged in relationship, people must know the truth that God freely gives the Twin Flame to each. This gift from God is an expression given from the beginning. Remember the bursting out from the sparks of the divine?

This is the divine gift given by God to each person at the moment of Creation.

Our purpose in the project that is this book is to help people remember the truth—that this is their divine gift.

Many know about the concept of Twin Flames and have the longing. Now it is for them to know the truth, that from God's pouring forth, they can receive the bliss and Love with their Twin Flame.

SHANNA: Thank you, my precious Pra.

CIRCLE OF LIGHT
SPIRITUAL CENTER

If one wishes to truly learn more about Twin
Flames, the most elevated, prolific and detailed
information with which I am familiar is in the
Messages from God received at Circle of Light
Spiritual Center in the years 2000 forward.
Though the spiritual center is no longer as
active, much of this information is still available
on the Circle of Light website
(www.circleoflight.net).

Highly recommended are the two published
volumes entitled *Say YES to Love, God Explains
SoulMates and Say YES to Love, God Unveils
SoulMate Love and Sacred Sexuality.* The
extremely important Messages from God which
these contain were brought through Yael Powell
and her Twin Flame, Doug, in that period, and
there has been nothing quite equaling them of
which I am aware. I had the honor at that time

of transcribing, editing and compiling this material into books. It was in this same period that I had my own early experiences during my meditations with my beloved Twin Flame, Pra.

We are hopeful that these two books will soon be reprinted and made more available. In the meantime, the best source is used bookstores or the COL website. There is also a mailing list on the website. Messages from the original works are sent to the people on the mailing list regularly.

YAEL AND DOUG POWELL

The story of how Yael and Doug came together is sweet and carries the stamp of the *irresistible magnetism* of Twin Flames. In October of 1986, Doug was living alone in a house that he had built in Eureka Springs, Arkansas. The house was struck by lightning one evening and burned to the ground. Following this event, Doug moved temporarily into the home of close friends who were travelling. He was grateful for the space and was caring for their dog, but he was also feeling alone and miserable. The house was solar powered, and the wood stove for winter had not yet been installed. He was cold and feeling homeless. He prayed to God, "God, I really want to go home."

The following weekend was the yearly gathering of the Midwest SUFI camp in a location in Oklahoma, west of Fayetteville, Arkansas, where Yael lived. Doug made arrangements to go with a friend from Eureka Springs. At the same time, a friend of Yael's in Fayetteville said to her, "I'm going to kidnap you and take you to SUFI camp today." That was a miraculous offer because at that time, Yael who suffered most of her life from a disease of the spine (ankylosing spondylitis) was in bed the greater part of the day with her hips elevated on an air mattress and her head and shoulders on the floor. She only got out of bed for brief periods each day. She did take a short drive around the block in her car every day to maintain her contact with the outside world, but she needed a home health care nurse to come in and help with cooking and necessities.

Nevertheless, this friend was as good as his word. He recruited some helpers, and they put Yael's bed in the back of a van and took her to the gathering. At the SUFI conference, she was placed on her mattress on the stage behind the teacher who was leading the session.

Doug noticed her immediately. He recalls that one of the SUFI people from the camp was giving her a lot of attention, and Doug felt pangs of jealousy! He had the thought, "Get away from her!" The lunch period took place in a different location, and Yael's friends had carried her there with one walking on either side, lifting her by her arms. She was seated with her lunch and talking to a man Doug knew. He recalls that he could not take his eyes off of her, as he ate his lunch three tables away.

He quickly finished his meal and hurried over to her table. "Hey, aren't you going to introduce me?" he asked his friend. Yael and Doug exchanged a brief conversation, but soon it was time to go back to the main presentation room. Again, Yael was settled in her bed on the stage behind the teacher, but this time, Doug sat beside her bed with her. They couldn't really speak to each other, as the teacher was giving a talk only about ten feet away. They spent the three hours of the presentation looking in each other's eyes, without saying anything. Doug recalls falling totally in love with her and feels that their connection was sealed immediately. This was especially interesting since Doug describes himself at that time as a "playboy," seldom staying long in a romantic relationship. Yael herself had been in a semi-serious relationship with another man.

Yael did give Doug her phone number, but since he did not write it down, she later admitted that she did not expect to hear from him again. (He had memorized it.) She left with the people who brought her, returning to her home in Fayetteville in public housing. Doug stayed at the camp and participated in the events of the following day. During that day, Yael was always on his mind. When, at the end of the events, the person sharing a ride home with Doug had a change of plans, Doug drove to Fayetteville, found a phone booth and called Yael. He asked if he could come to see her. She said she would love that and gave him directions.

Doug moved in with her for the rest of her life. They stayed in Fayetteville through the winter, and in the spring, Doug moved her to Eureka Springs, his hometown. He built a complex ramp on the home they were to occupy so that she could get in and out of the house. It was the first of many accommodations Doug built to enable Yael to expand her social life.

Her Fayetteville friends were very concerned about the move, as they felt protective of Yael, and she had established a strong support system around her. However, a personal event occurred on December 14, two months after they had met, which cemented the pathway of both of their lives. As they both awoke during one night, they spontaneously spoke vows to each other, though they were half asleep. Later on, they asked each other, "Did we get married last night?" It was a Sunday. The couple dressed in white and went out on what was a weekly outing to a little restaurant for brunch (almost the only time they ever socialized, for Yael's ability to move about was so compromised). They told their friends at the restaurant that they had gotten married, and the restaurant treated them to brunch.

Yael and Doug consecrated their marriage several other times through spiritual ceremonies, once with a large gathering of friends and more than once with a vow renewal. Though Yael and Doug had to surmount many challenges in their relationship, complicated by the intensity and the complexity of her physical condition, they never left each other's side. Doug cared for her through many illnesses and was a devoted life-long caregiver. She returned to God in January 2018. Their powerful attraction reflected their creation by God at the Moment of Creation as a Twin Flame couple.

THE MESSAGES FROM GOD

When she first started "channeling," many years ago, Yael received messages from different sources and different beings, including from the Devas and Nature Spirits. These communications took different forms, some as poetry and even as drawings. At the time that I, Shanna, arrived at Circle of Light in December 2000, Yael had filled **eighty** hand-written spiral notebooks with Messages she had received. These Messages still reside in a bookcase at Circle of Light.

At that time, this beautiful being, whose heart was so open and whose challenging life as a transformer in a disabled body here in physicality she had gracefully accepted with patience and fortitude, had been receiving a Message from God during her meditation every day. In her modest humility, she still referred to them as "Meditations," but she was soon instructed to entitle them The Messages from God, and indeed, they came through her in the form of our Beloved Creator speaking to humanity in the first person. Many of the Messages of this period were specifically about Twin Flames. Messages on other topics also made frequent reference to the Twin Flame phenomenon.

Through the Messages, God explained to Yael that she and Doug were "original" Twin Flames who had agreed to come together on Earth at this time to introduce this information to humanity. After I arrived at Circle of Light, many of the God Messages contained similar comments about my experiences with my Twin Flame, Pra, as well. We were told that we represented two differing versions of Twin Flames—a couple who were both in embodiment on Earth and a couple with one in embodiment and the other Twin in Spirit on the "other side." We had agreed to undertake this assignment of bringing the truth of Twin Flames to our brothers and sisters on Earth.

TWIN FLAMES AND CREATION

To share with you information about the Moment of Creation and the amazing key role that Twin Flames play in our Creation according to the Messages from God, I will allow the Messages from God speak for themselves. I will quote directly. Most of these quotations come from two published books, Say YES to Love, God Explains SoulMates; and *Say YES to Love, God Unveils SoulMate Love and Sacred Sexuality*, but there are also quotes from earlier unpublished Messages from God.[4]

This assignment has been given to me to assist all of us to open our hearts and to remember, at a very profound level, knowledge that each of us carries deeply within, but which we have temporarily "forgotten." As you read,

you will each receive this in individual ways.
Some may receive through a resonance created
by a word or words or a vibration; images may
arise as the material is shared. Some of you will
feel your intuition activated as you read the
quotations from God. Others may have
experiences of sudden remembrance or
awakening, or what Pra described to us as the
"felt sense." Please be open to any of these
experiences and more yet.

Some of you have touched this information
before. To others it will be completely new.
Perhaps you have read something about Soul
Mates from time to time but doubted the
possibility of drawing your Twin Flame to
yourself. It is such powerful information that
some will turn away, feeling that the depth of the
beauty opened here cannot possibly reside in the
challenging third dimensional world in which we
now live on Earth. Others may feel that they are
not worthy of being with their Twin Flame. It is
true that our egos will not welcome this
information.

As you will note, God tells us that this
information will be our main assignment in the
years to come. My humble task at this moment is
to once again plant seeds, through this book, in
the garden of our hearts, as directed by the
Messages from God. This truth will gradually

open in our hearts and then reveal itself to each of us in different ways in our daily lives in the times to come.

This leads me to a comment I am guided to express about the substantial literature online and in books about SoulMates and Twin Flames. Much of it will be very different from what you are reading in this book, lighter in content and some of it ego based. If you are exploring this territory, you will indeed find many different versions of SoulMate stories—fiction, "channeled" and autobiographical. All of these expressions are introductions to the truth that is being opened for us.

People receive at the vibrational level to which they are currently attuned. The topic is now being opened on the planet. We are encouraged to participate at whatever level we are able. The truth will unfold in its time and in the meantime, any presentation that encourages people to open their hearts to God, to Love and to their beautiful Twin serves a useful purpose.

Please note that in the Messages from God, the terms "SoulMate" and "TwinFlame" are used interchangeably. Though one can find many definitions in other spiritual sources, especially online, citing differences between layers and levels of SoulMates, Soul Family and other terms, this is not true in the Circle of Light material. <u>Whether the term Twin Flame or the term SoulMate is used, the Messages from God are always referring specifically to the Twin Flame,</u> the original creation of the two who are one, Divine Masculine and Divine Feminine, at the Moment of Creation.

I remind you that all of the following excerpts presented as GOD SPEAKS were taken from meditations through Yael Powell, exactly as they were received in the early years of the 2000's. They are presented here again in this form so that more people may access them. Commentaries by ShannaPra are marked SP at the end.

***

As you read the following direct quotations from The Messages from God, please ask to open your heart as much as possible. Ask to experience a direct, intuitive understanding of the information that is being given.

Imagine yourself being held lovingly in the arms of our Beloved Mother/Father God and spoken to personally and intimately.

We are told that humanity is now on the path to being sufficiently individuated and spiritually aware to be given detailed information about our true origin. It is a great honor for humanity that we are now given this information.

Our Beloved Creator speaks to us personally, intimately and passionately through these Messages. Not only do we receive amazing and revelatory information; we receive the deep and eternal Love of the Father/Mother God for Its children. (SP).

GOD SPEAKS:

"My beautiful ones, can you picture a cell of My heart? I want you to absorb this question. I want you to stretch to encompass this thought, this wholeness (for 'thought' certainly does not contain it!) I want you to do your best, at the highest level possible for you at this time, to understand this.

"This is who you are. You are a

cell in My heart, the heart of the Creator of All That Is. The One, the Alpha and Omega, and everything in between—the forces of Light and Love that, moving together, have manifested all life, all worlds, all beauty and filled each and every one of these creations with grace and with the power to transform.

"... your SoulMate is the other half of the cell [of my heart]. Together you are one cell of My heart.

"You are at the center of Creation. You, together, exist as cause, not as effect. You are the beginning of Love. You are the foundation of My being.

"You are My heart.

"While you cannot understand this with your mind—for your minds are far too limited to hold this—there are keys that will reawaken this knowledge in you. These keys are living energies, energies that will affect you, bless you and grow you. They are energies most of all that will reawaken you to what you know."

"This will now be your human course of study in the next few decades.

"Out of this study will come your full awakening as conscious participants in the communion that is Creation. This beautiful ballet that is life, that is Creation, is being called Sacred Geometry, and humanity is beginning to awaken and become aware of its study. This study will be the platform from which I launch you into your becoming the conscious heart of God. Co-creators. Beings of greatest Love known throughout the All for what you truly are.

"Once humanity accepts the path of the Soul Mate [Twin Flame], the code will be activated. Humankind will know. My heart will become fully conscious.

"Oh, My beloved humanity! Would that you could know how much I love you, how deeply I know you, how perfectly you are created. In this age I give you the precious mirror of your own divine Love— your SoulMate [Twin Flame]. Not as a figure rising above you as an example. Rather, as the complete experience of total and personal immersion in perfect divine Love.

"I ask you now, this very moment, to invite Me. Invite Me into you, into your life, into your world. And know as you do this that absolutely everything in your life will be illuminated in My

presence. All things within you that
may be blocking your awakening,
the recognition of your SoulMate,
or the perfect return to your
embodiment of Love will be
revealed."

Please stop at this moment. Pause and attune to
your feelings. Can you feel a truth, a beauty, a
personal "call" in these words? Do you feel an
urge to read them again in order to allow them to
penetrate your being? How can these words be
spoken to us by other than our beloved Creator?

Can we not assume that Our Beloved Creator
knows all aspects of our lives that have led to our
present moment? Is our Father-Mother-God not
completely cognizant of all that we have
experienced and aware of all that we long for?
Can we not be sure that each of us is completely
known, both in our individuation and in the
Oneness with God that we are? Each of us is
completely understood and deeply loved.

It is clear to our Creator that we desire to feel
with all our hearts the Love that is the true
nature of our being in God, and that up until
now, we have not been able to truly receive the
deepest import of this knowing about ourselves.
There is a divine patience and deep compassion

expressed in these Messages from God for each one of us, but also God's urgent desire for us to return to knowledge of WHO WE ARE and for us to receive the joy and gifts—especially the reunion with the Twin Flame—all that is waiting for us. (SP)

GOD SPEAKS:

"The first and foremost key in the Awakening of humanity is the SoulMate [TwinFlame].

"[This is] . . . the miracle for which all of your journeys have prepared you, all of your lives, all of your lessons, all of the things you have built and stored over the centuries (millennia!) in the special treasure chest of your Highest Self, awaiting the moment when all is ready.

"This is such a time. This I promise. Let this promise resonate in your heart, dear ones. Let it resonate until you can feel it cracking the shell that surrounds your heart. Let it resonate within you until you are aware of a corresponding resonance—your SoulMate [Twin Flame]."

This reference to "cracking the shell that surrounds your heart" occurs several times in the Messages from God and is important. Most of us have been participating in this adventure on Earth in physical embodiments for an extended time. The nature of the dream, the illusion, the creation that is life on Earth is such that we have often felt the need to guard our hearts and protect ourselves in various ways. Sometimes we are not even aware of how guarded we have kept our hearts. This protection with which we have felt necessary to surround ourselves, and which has become a habit of which we have often lost conscious awareness has blocked our access to many of the beautiful aspects of life that might be available to us.

Some of you may recall that before my Twin Flame, Pra, was revealed to me for the first time during my meditation, I was shown the image of a heavy metal garage door closing from top to bottom—an image that depicted my closed heart. I immediately understood the message. I knew that my heart had been closed. I had not been satisfied with the relationships I had been drawing to myself. This had, however, also caused me to develop a fear of relationship, so I had surrounded myself with even more self-protection.

Many of the relationships that I had experienced to this point in my life were not in alignment with what was now becoming my spiritual truth. I began to open my heart, little by little. As I immersed myself in the Twin Flame Messages from God, I opened ever more to a higher truth. This will happen for each of us.

God is now showing us that to return to the way God originally created us, we must *completely* open our hearts. The open heart and the giving of Love are the pathway to the Twin Flame. One of our tasks is to become aware of the many "protective" blocks we have held onto and thought forms that have kept our hearts closed, and to trust God and to make the choice to release them. As we are able to release all judgment and open our hearts, we will begin to feel "the spiritual signature" of the Twin. (SP)

GOD SPEAKS:

"This resonance of [an open] heart will become the spiritual signature, the vibrational statement of your truth. It is very important. Not only will you draw to you your SoulMate [Twin Flame]. You will also draw all the things that reflect who you are in the world. While this can be positive, it is secondary. The most important (oh, I can't possibly tell you how important!) is your resonance for your SoulMate [TwinFlame].

"Your SoulMate is not some random being whom you might find if you are lucky. <u>You will find your SoulMate. You cannot not find your SoulMate for you ARE your SoulMate, and your SoulMate is you.</u> Yes, you are individuals. And you are not. For as I have told you, <u>you are two parts of one cell in My heart.</u> Nothing can keep you apart."

The information in this last quotation, given very early (2001) in an unpublished Message from God, *contains the keys to a true understanding of the Twin Flame.* However, because on Earth we tend to think of ourselves as individuals, and independent of one another, most of us have difficulty in truly grasping the information that is given here.

From the viewpoint of our seemingly separate bodies, we struggle to comprehend the all-encompassing major spiritual concept that WE ARE really ALL ONE—multitudinous facets of one great being. And so does this related concept that we are always one with our Twin Flame (whom we cannot see) challenge our usual ways of seeing ourselves as individual and independent. The perspectives of duality and individuality are so present in Earth life that they lead us to constantly look outside of ourselves for everything—for Love, for partners and ultimately, for the SoulMate or Twin Flame.

Yet, the sentences, *"You ARE your SoulMate, and your SoulMate is you"* and *"you are two parts of one cell in My heart"* are absolutely seminal to an understanding of Twin Flames.

Add to that another challenge to our Earthly minds—the possibility that though our Twin Flame is always a part of us, the Love that is the Twin Flame Love may express through others, those around us who are playing an important role in our lives.

Do hold all of this lightly in your heart, as you

also hold the beginnings of any remembering you may begin to experience of the Twin Flame. There is more of the story to be told. (SP)

GOD SPEAKS:

"Every beauty is within you! Every spark of life, every capacity for love.

"And built into your very beings on every level is the essential flow of the energy of life. Now you will find it in your fullness, which is your awakening with your soulmate [Twin Flame].

"Why do I not say it is in 'finding' your soulmate [Twin Flame]? Why do I say awakening? Because your soulmate never is apart from you. It is impossible for you to be separated. For dear ones, in truth, you are one being.

"You are one being <u>temporarily</u>

<u>unable to see the other part of yourselves,</u> even though that part is right in front of you.

"How can this be? How can I say such a thing when whole lives are given to the search for this soulmate? How can I expect you to believe such a thing when people live alone and die, all the while wishing for that soulmate?

"I know it will be difficult to believe at first, but over time you will come to understand this truth. You are separated by vibrational disparity—the inability of the 'apparatus' of the physical vehicle to be aware of the subtle world around you. <u>This disparity is changing</u>."

Despite the obvious confusion and negativity we still observe in the third dimensional world in which we live, this higher vibrational shift in which life is moving faster and lighter is very actively upon us. *Our beloved Creator is "calling us Home."* We have nearly completed the goals of our journey of individuation.

Of course, we continue to walk in and identify with the dream world we have created, desiring to return it to a world of Love and only Love. At the same time, as we feel the call in our hearts, our physical vehicles are becoming "less physical," and we are reaching ever higher for our original truth that brings us closer to our reunion with our Twin Flame as we were created. (SP)

GOD SPEAKS:

"Now, even though people look solid here, they are not. And even though you believe that each and every individual here is an entirely separate being, they are not. <u>Humanity is all one heart. My heart.</u> You have grasped this understanding about past lives, that you are one soul having pieces of yourself experiencing different things at the same time, for in truth your lives are all happening at once.

"The same is true of the SoulMate relationship. It is essentially the two of you peering down into matter and interacting with the rest of My heart in this growth experience, this individualization.

"As your SoulMate is brought into embodiment, it means that your heart is pure enough, loving enough, to have this reflected to you in form.

"As this beautiful expression of your loving heart comes ever more fully into embodiment, of course, an energy exchange takes place. This energy exchange nourishes you and nourishes your SoulMate!

"Ultimately, you become One Heart together. The moment you do so, that cell in My heart is 'switched on.' That cell in My heart becomes the 'Light Cell' it is meant to be, able to create Love and to move it by Will, together.

"Dear ones, what you call light is actively moving Love. It is Love vibrating. It is this giving forth, this movement of Love that is the foundation of Creation. The substance of all things is Love.

"So, it is your first step to reawaken to the presence of your SoulMate, who is with you. (There is no way they cannot be—you are one cell). Then once you are awakened to each other's presence again, together you will process and utilize all the learning that your own heart cells have brought into your being.

"There is nothing more important than awakening to your SoulMate, for in this, you will remember the full truth of your being. And so remembering, you will awaken to Our communion. Only the experience can convey this beauty. Yet every step of the way, as SoulMates awaken in the remembrance of Love, will bring Me fully into your experience. Relating to your SoulMate is the next closest thing to your heritage of communion in Me. Through your SoulMate awakening, you will prepare yourselves to directly experience My Love and Our partnership.

"So whether you are with someone or not, whether you believe that person could possibly be your SoulMate or not, I ask you to trust in Me. Trust Me to set up your soul reunion, to invoke the full memory of the truth of your being, to put forth your heart resonance, the vibrational signature of who

you really are. Then make every
decision based in this truth."

In the quotes from the Messages from God that
follow, God makes it absolutely clear that there
was intentional divine purpose in our long and
arduous "travels" that followed our birth at the
Moment of Creation. Our voyages were
anticipated, necessary for our individuation, and
we undertook each adventure that God asked us
to take to gain our individuation, <u>regardless of
its possible outcome.</u> This means we followed the
path we were assigned, even when it *appeared* to
result in "separation from God."

As stated earlier in this writing, it is my
understanding that as we explore the many
different possible pathways we may have taken
as Twin Flame Sparks of God since the Moment
of Creation, it is very important that we always
know in our hearts that any suggestion that we
ever truly "separated" at any time from our
Creator speaks of a condition that is impossible.

If we were ever truly separated from our
Father Mother God, the Source of our life, we
would no longer exist. Any separation which is
mentioned is a <u>seeming</u> separation—a separation
in our thought, in our consciousness, an idea of
separation, someone's description (their idea!) of
a separation. God's Creations are infinite and

can never be separated from their Source, our Beloved Mother Father God. However, there are many ways in which it APPEARED that we had been separated from God. (SP)

GOD SPEAKS:

"Now I have explained to you before about the problem that we had in the beginning. It was this. You loved Me so much (and I, you) that you could not stay away from Me. You could not become individualized children of God because you would blissfully sink back into the Love that we are.

"Thus, you began as a cell in My heart, so much a part of Me that there was no real distinction between us. We could not truly relate to each other. If you moved away from Me, the moment you turned back and looked at Me, you automatically came rushing back. You were not co-creators. You did not have Will of your own. Thus came the journey. 'Leaving the Garden' is the perfect description. But now, dear ones, you are coming back! And what is the key to the Garden gate? Knowledge of the SoulMate [Twin Flame].

"Now, as Creation moved—outward, inward and multidimensionally—each cell of My heart, each of you as SoulMate pairs, also burst forth in an explosion of joy and excitement that seeded yourselves all the way along the path of individualization. In other words, you placed pieces of yourselves along the way. The goal was for you to gain enough individuality that you could live within Me, but not merge your consciousness with Me.

"I Am calling you Home. It is time to recognize your own heart.

"Nothing can keep you from each other. It is a requisite of your opening heart.

"In truth, you are one. Once you get to the point of real access to your heart, you will see your SoulMate.

"Elevation is the process by which the truth of Love is understood. It is the speeding up of vibration until your consciousness is vibrating fast enough to mesh with the truth of Love. Life on the physical plane, of course, is vibrating very slowly. So to embrace the truth of Love, to understand it, you must vibrate fast enough to connect with it. All of your prayers, affirmations and meditations are for this purpose. However, the fastest way to elevate the speed or the rate of vibration of your consciousness is the reunion with your SoulMate.

"Because together you are the union of the forces of Creation, you will bring these energies back into presence in the world. Using them, letting the Divine Masculine and Divine Feminine return to Earth in you, you can and must change everything. In your Love you will lift the Earth and all the beauty upon and within it back into the vibration of Love."

One of the most inspiring and hopeful aspects of the words God shares here is the promise that we can affect in a positive way the world of the "dream," "the illusion," the world which we have created here through the mind, the world in which we walk on Earth. As Twin Flames come together at all levels, the power and purity of the Love of reuniting with one's Twin, the way one was created originally by God, *is so strong that it greatly amplifies the power of Love itself on Earth, and makes all things possible.* There is a strong desire when Twins unite to give to the whole, to brothers and sisters everywhere. The

Love that is the natural essence of us is greatly amplified and the natural inclination is to send it forth for the healing of all humanity. (SP)

GOD SPEAKS:

"Right now in human awakening there is nothing more important than opening to the SoulMate. I can promise you that as soon as you experience the Love of your SoulMate [Twin Flame], you will see everything else correctly. You will understand. To put this "biblically," to come back to the Garden, Adam and Eve must find each other, for that garden is made for two. That is how you already exist! Your SoulMate is part of you. This is a FACT. Twin Flames. Two halves of one whole. Two sides of One heart. Two reflections of One consciousness.

"The forgetting time is OVER. To find your individuality, you have taken many forms, separated from the truth so you would believe you were alone. <u>This was an important part of a</u> <u>very important plan.</u> But at the end of the "involution" of your journey of individuality, we agreed that you would know it was time to turn back toward Me— when you were united with your SoulMate [Twin Flame]."

Here again we have reference to the need we had to individuate, find our individuality, an "important part of a very important plan." Humanity has been on a long, long journey (though, in truth, time does not exist). Many of us feel in our souls the deep fatigue, the seemingly unanswered longing of our hearts to finish what has been a challenging, endless period of exploration. We feel the call of HOME. (SP)

GOD SPEAKS:

"As you have learned, you only have one SoulMate [Twin Flame]. This SoulMate is the other half of your great and glorious eternal being. This SoulMate is the other half, with you, of the cell of My heart. This being is that cell born into manifestation at the Moment of Creation, for in that moment I became manifested. I became the expanding Creation, of which you are the heart.

"Until that moment I was still consciousness. A pool of Love. But there rose in Me the great desire to give forth that Love. This desire grew within Me until it burst forth and, crackling with the energy of My longing, it became two things instead of one. It became the giver and the one who receives. Out of this moment and this action upon the deep, the action of Will, of thought, upon the ocean of My Love, My Love brought forth All That Is. All That Is in relationship.

"All That Is in relationship is forever comprised of the energies of the 'First Split,' where that which receives became the Divine Feminine and that which gives, the Divine Masculine. Thus, everything in Creation is now and forever the relationship of these two energies, including the nature of the cells of My heart."

The so-called "First Split" refers to the creation by God at the Moment of Creation of the two aspects of our Mother/Father God—Divine Feminine and Divine Masculine. This was God's pattern, God's template for all of Creation. This became extended throughout Creation as we undertook our exploratory voyages into individuation. This is described in many ways throughout the Circle of Light Messages and other spiritual writing (see below). In the words of the Messages from God, *"the embodiment of My masculine energy, the energy of going forth that brought Creation into being. The spark that rose within Me, in the void, the urge to explore, to reach forth, to discover. Pure decision, direction, goal: the arrow flying forth, bringing life out of the void.*

"The Divine Feminine, the receptive womb waiting to receive, waiting to wrap life in Love, to nurture, honor, to bless, to love by taking in, to love by knowing that which is loved so deeply that it lives within, to be the receiver, and from this gift, to bring forth new life."

The tension AND the balance between the two aspects, masculine and feminine, is often described as providing the energy of ongoing creation—that which is active and that which is receptive. (SP)

GOD SPEAKS:

"Knowing that it was our goal to relate (the whole reason for Creation), you, the great beings who are My heart, chose to move away from Me, to individuate so you could become your own identity. So (pay attention), you turned and dove outward into Creation, <u>moving down into density to gain distance from Me.</u> It was the only way we could do it. As you dove, you looked out at all of these levels you went through on your outward journey. Every time you looked, a piece of your attention/consciousness took up residence at that level in order to explore it. These are what we call your incarnations or personalities."

Through religious teachings and spiritual teachings as well, we have been chastised for our supposed "separation from God," creating concepts of sin, guilt, and diminishing our pure and natural feelings of Love for ourselves and for our Creator. In the Messages from God, it becomes evident that the individuation was an essential part of the plan for our creation, which gave God, our Creator, the opportunity to experience all the multitudinous facets of Self. No one knew all the possible ramifications of that path, but everyone might imagine that our Creator could and would call us "Home" when the moment was right.

"It was our goal to relate—the whole reason for Creation!"

Again, however, we must reiterate that never were we truly separated from Mother Father God, without whose Love and intention for us, we would not have continued in existence. (SP)

GOD SPEAKS:

"This Earth level was the end of the dive, if you want to look at it this way. So on all these various levels of experience, there are pieces of your consciousness all existing at once, and all in contact with the higher self.

" However, things became very dense here at this last level of your manifested lives, and you lost contact with all of the other pieces of consciousness. It can be likened to being on a Star Trek away mission. You are down here on the planet. You've lost communication with the ship. You think you are alone, and you're caught in a 'temporal anomaly,' so it seems you have been here forever.

"All the while, the crew is aware of everything you do and is

desperately trying to get a message
through with instructions on how
to get back to the ship."

So now our challenge is: how to return Home?
Here we are, living within a self-created
illusion on Earth in which Love has been clouded
over by our forgetting who we are. We have
seemingly reached the farthest point (in density)
in which we can continue to individuate and
extend "Love," and still maintain our
consciousness, our vibration as a God being, a
child of God exploring for God. It is imperative
that we find ways to raise our vibration to be
able to give and receive Love in order to continue
to the next phases of our evolution homeward.

God gives us an important answer. <u>This is the
moment when the reconnection with the Twin
Flame becomes the most important spiritual
task.</u> It is not the only way we can elevate our
vibration, but it does quickly and easily provide
the amplification and power of Love, the
energetic force that can shift our perceptions/our
perspective to seeing right through the illusion to
the Real of who we are. It purifies and
strengthens our hearts for our return journey
Home to God. This is not really a physical
journey, but even more challenging, it is a
vibrational journey and a perceptual shift in

which by our living our truth, <u>all before us shifts to the Real of God.</u> (SP)

GOD SPEAKS:

"Now, your SoulMate [Twin Flame] is the great, vast being who is huge, as are you. While both of you have had your attention placed outward on these personalities through your many incarnations to build your separate identities, you are still who you are. Your SoulMate is still vast and powerful and so are you. It is this energy, this real fullness of your SoulMate you are returning to. For the personalities have served their purpose.

"They have created many experiences and strong and individualized beings of the two of you. Now it is time for the two great energies that you are to reunite.

"Dear ones, there is no way to fully explain to you the truth of this vastness of your being. Suffice it to say that the two of you, Twin Rays, great SoulMates [Twin Flames] of the "First Split" of My Being, will now send forth the truth of your beings. <u>This truth will pour through every one of your many personalities or incarnations, and all of them will recognize the truth of who they really are and call forth the connection with the true, vast, great and powerful fullness of their true being.</u>

"In other words, dear ones, every personality being expressed by your great self will now be lifted into the truth. As the great being pours through you more and more and more, <u>the personalities you were will be lifted up vibrationally and expanded until they become a part of the Great SoulMate Union.</u>

"This is why I have said to you that your SoulMate will manifest through the person you are with. For I guarantee that <u>in every incarnation, every person you have ever been with is a piece of your SoulMate [TwinFlame].</u>

"Everyone. And in every incarnation your SoulMate has been reflecting to you your state of consciousness. It is always your SoulMate, wearing different personalities to mirror to you the state of your Love. It is only because you are way down in this density that you can believe that it is different people."

There are several concepts here that require most of us to open our minds wide, wide, wide, and take a leap in consciousness. We have developed a particular way of perceiving as we have traveled through the many adventures that eventually led to life on Earth as we are now experiencing it. Especially since we have been on Earth in individual bodies, we have seen every thought, every experience as separate from everyone else. That way of perceiving that which is around us might be thought of as perceiving with a "separated consciousness" (me, myself and I or ego).

That is, despite exposure to beautiful teachings from our Creator, Masters, Archangels which assure us that *WE ARE ALL ONE, we still view our brothers and sisters with whom we interact in Earth life as completely separate entities from ourselves.* In this "separation consciousness," we are often "at war" with each other—being competitive, comparative, judging and striving for independence from each other.

Now, in these Messages, God is affirming for us that which we have been told in many other teachings—that this is both an erroneous and unproductive way to view our lives. Every being "in a body" with whom each one of us has ever interacted on our journeys is a part of that being's own self, is a piece of our very own Twin Flame. We were created as the Two Who Are One, and we have all been creating and playing dramas with ourselves through the eons of our travels. (SP)

GOD SPEAKS:

"If you are cells of My heart

which contain only one positive and one negative charge, then everyone to whom you relate can only be the other half of that cell of My heart. Once you truly understand the truth of your SoulMate [Twin Flame], you will see it perfectly. If your SoulMate is ever and always with you, yet you must learn how to be individualized through the illusion and the return to Love, the only way it could be done is for each of you to wear many personalities, each helping the other to grow into full consciousness of Love as individualized cells of My heart.

"Many of you have had the experience of meeting someone and knowing his/her spirit. And feeling this, you could have sworn, "this was it"—only to find that your personalities could not get along at all. This was because you did know them. Their essence was your

SoulMate [Twin Flame] but you were not open enough to Love to draw in the truth of your SoulMate. For as you now see, it is only as you become Love that Love will become what you see and what you live.

"As you awaken, you open your beings, Your SoulMate manifests with you, still as a personality. As you expand, more and more of the light that is your great SoulMate self pours into the two of you. You become less and less defined on this physical plane as your beings become more and more comprised of the great Love that you are.

"I ask you to completely trust the truth of Love. That truth is your SoulMate [Twin Flame], one being forever, wearing many personalities.

"Together you are a cell in My very heart. I ask you to know that the purity of Love in your heart and your call for your SoulMate pours the golden light of your highest self down into your life, and the more you can accept it as your truth, the more you will see it in your world. Your SoulMate will manifest ever more clearly as you are clear and able to see Love. Your SoulMate [Twin Flame] has manifested that personality you see before you. Absolutely. In reflection of your own Love."

We are told, "Your SoulMate [Twin Flame] will manifest ever more clearly as you are clear and able to see Love." Another way to say this is: your Twin Flame will appear in your life to the exact extent that your heart is open. If your heart is a little bit open, the being before you will reflect a small degree of loving openness. As you are able to open your heart wider and wider and pour Love upon that person, he/she will appear to transform and become ever more appealing to you, ever more "spiritual," more loving, more, more, more. (SP)

GOD SPEAKS:

"Trust your SoulMate's existence and manifestation ever more fully in your life, completely. Live by this trust without question. Look for the truth of both of you in your partner's eyes. <u>And know, dear ones, that you do not need </u>to go anywhere to find your SoulMate. You have never been apart. If you are with someone, begin right now to see the truth. Begin to love so purely that the highest level of your being can be delivered to both of you. Live expectantly and greet every increase in Love and energy with celebration and joy. Then turn together and begin generating Love for the world that the clouds of illusion for everyone will be melted away in the sunshine of your Love.

"The greatest key for the reclamation of the SoulMate [Twin

Flame] Love is giving. This you can do no matter what the illusion has placed before you. If you can't see this possibility in your partner, start speaking to his spirit, for I promise that your spirits are SoulMates, are glory and communion of Love. As you open your heart, you will see your SoulMate. This I promise you.

"So all who are looking, must look within themselves, that they will be clear enough to receive the Love being sent from the highest level of their beings, the SoulMate as Divine Masculine or Divine Feminine. If you can 'unfreeze' yourself, your SoulMate will follow. And should you find yourself with a seemingly recalcitrant personality, I ask you to not be fooled by appearance. Know that Love will find a way. Your SoulMate's truth will be seen by you to the degree that you are able to see it in yourself, to give it to your partner, and to see it as their highest truth. Remember, Love is expansion.

"Giving is Love's truth.

"So as you give Love to your SoulMate, the Love you give *does* return to you tenfold. What does this mean? It means that as human beings in your completion with your SoulMate, you become a great generating station for Love. You together give birth to more and more and more Love! Can you feel this? You give to your beloved – whether or not they are giving to you, and you are rewarded with ten times the Love pouring into you that you can then direct.

"We have spoken many times, dear ones, of moving from the ego to the heart. We have noted that the ego is ever seeking to GET

while the heart wants to GIVE.
Now that you are understanding
ever larger truths, you can see that
there is even more at stake in this
shift. For beloved ones, now you
understand the truth of SoulMates
and the fact that it is time for your
reunion. You are understanding
also that your open heart is what
draws your SoulMate ever more
fully into your life, and now, dear
ones, I am showing you that Love
can be generated through the
sacred SoulMate union and that
this very Love will heal the fabric
of the world. As you create new
Love through Lovemaking and send
it forth, beloved ones, it literally
"repairs the tissue" of the entire
physical universe, anywhere such
repair is needed. So if you realize
that Giving generates a tenfold
return of Love and that you can
send forth this Love for the healing
of the world—think how quickly

everything can be changed!

GOD SPEAKS:

"Thus, when My children first inhabited Earth, it was the Garden of Eden. Long before any civilizations had come and gone, there were only Twin Flames, going forth to create and naming what they brought forth. They experienced a communion of spirit and being that is so far beyond your current experience that your most exalted words will barely begin to convey it.

"It was truly the Forces of Creation moving together in true LoveMaking that brought forth the idea of the world and filled it in.

"You have been perfecting your individuality. You have been becoming your own being. So just to

be sure there were no accidents,
you and your SoulMate have been
separated. This was the result of
our mutual choice. When your
vibrational reality slipped further
into density than planned, it was
obvious that you could make some
big mistakes if you had the mature
power of your SoulMate
relationship, for together, you are
the force of creation. As you chose
to believe in darkness as well as
light, you lost your ability to
remember your SoulMate."

We are being told that the strongest spiritual
position available to us at this moment is the
reconnection of Twin Flames, whose coming
together opens the possibility for the giving of
Love at the level of purity and power that we had
at the original Moment of Creation.

We, Lightworkers, can gain reassurance about
our dedication to our spiritual path on Earth—
despite what we see around us in the illusion
world—from the fact that we are now given the
possibility of experiencing true Twin Flame
reunion, right where we are on our path. We can

also imagine that this grand gift of Twin Flame reunion, with its potential for shifting our world, would not be offered to us if there were not confidence directly from our Creator, and among the Masters and Beings in the higher dimensions, the confidence that we are ready to return to the experience of Sacred Love. (SP)

GOD SPEAKS:

"Now here we are today. You have gained the individuality that was the goal. My children now complete, ready to go forth to create.

"So now, at this breathtaking moment, the memory of your SoulMate is being returned to you. Oh, My beloveds, please open your heart! Can you feel all that this means? Into your consciousness I now place the knowledge of your completion, your power, and your place in Creation. In this revelation *I am also giving to you the way to*

correct every mistake, to transform the results of every misunderstanding through all time. And, I am fulfilling your heart's deepest desire.

"Having said this, I now must say with great force, <u>you must not put any of your attention on the darkness that is being exposed.</u> Especially as you reclaim your power and move toward your SoulMate, you must take full responsibility for the creative power now being activated. Knowing that your attention united with your SoulMate is the power of all Creation born in you as your heritage, obviously you cannot put your attention on negativity. You can acknowledge what is really happening (the increasing light exposing the darkness) and you then must send Love.

"And know that you can easily walk through anything that is happening in the world as long as your vision stays, unwavering on Love.

"I love you. Passionately. When you understand the passion of God, you will understand yourselves. I can promise you that even those who seem so soft and gentle and full of sweet light ARE living in a passionate exaltation of life. Yet it is expressed perfectly through their being. Of course, as you know, each and every one of My Creations is unique. Each and every one of you has a place in Creation, a role to fill, an expansion of Love that no one else can accomplish. So My precious ones, please cherish your expression of Love and vow to bring it forth now."

A very important topic for us to understand as we open to our Twin Flame is the power of our sexuality. God discusses this in detail in the second half of the volume, Say YES to Love, God Unveils SoulMate Love and Sacred Sexuality.

***

As an example of the wisdom we are being given at this time, and to open the topic of our powerful sexuality as TwinFlames, we are now guided to offer to you here <u>the full Message</u> entitled "The Atomic Power of SoulMate Love and the Keys to Using it." This appears in the second half of the book, God Unveils SoulMate Love and Sacred Sexuality (pp. 183–195). At the time that this message was channeled through Yael, God called it "the most powerful message ever to be given to humanity."

It is lengthy, esoteric and exciting. Do not be discouraged if you do not understand some of it. God has told us that Twin Flames and Sacred Sexuality will be our greatest study project in the times to come. We will be guided, instructed.

We suggest that you not embark upon reading this Message unless you have full time and space to digest its contents. You can always skip forward in the book and return here at a later time if you wish. (SP)

GOD SPEAKS:

THE ATOMIC POWER OF SOULMATE LOVE

AND THE KEYS TO USING IT

GOD— "The most powerful Message ever to be given to humanity."

"I want to take your hand and write upon the starry heavens the truth of My Creation. I want to lift your eyes, My precious children. I want to show you how to read these messages, washing your beautiful faces with the winds of truth. *I want to show you that whatever you believe lives without, is truly*

only what lives within. I believe
that finally you are awake enough
to see it.

"For you to see this starry
message will take everything you
have learned from me. For this,
dear ones, this is *The Shift.* While
it may take you many years to
finally see it, *I now plant the seeds
of human destiny, the glorious
seeds of Love. I now say to you that
within you lies not only the hope of
the Earth and all of its life upon it.
Also with you lies the hope of Love.*
Dear ones, I will show you that you
can be within and you can be
without and in each and every
place you choose to be; you are the
creator, for you are My children. I
have said this continually. It is
time for you to learn what this
means.

"First, we must speak again

about the route Home, and I must tell you (as if you did not already know) that none of these things are the whole picture. Yet with every step you are seeing more. Every time that you align yourselves with Me, My beloved ones, I am made whole. I have missed you! I have missed you, as you would miss the heart beating in your chest! Of course, should your heart stop, your body would cease to exist in its current form. Likewise, it is with My heart, dear ones. For while you travel through this journey of independence from Me, there is a hollow where the richness of My awakened heart would be. So you can see how ready for you I am. The waiting will soon be over.

"Sacred Sexuality. SoulMates. To you these words are still about human relationships. Yet I want to show you that *they are about much more*, for in these two things is the key—the key to the door of the mansions of God which is where you are meant to live.

"Sacred Sexuality. This is the piece we will speak of the most, for you are understanding the SoulMates. That is written in your heart. It is written in your genes. At night it sings to you its song of your destiny if only you will remember. And when you allow yourselves to hear the song, you know that you MUST have your SoulMate. And when you *know*, with absolute certainty, your SoulMate will appear. But such certainty must mean that you are willing to live the Fairy Tale. Of course, the very reason that every fairy tale and all the myths are so popular, enduring for centuries, living in your minds, your books, your movies is that they are REAL.

There is an archetype in these tales that is the blueprint for life in this world. The time is now for bringing these stories into "concrete" reality (a conflict in terms!).

"In the fairy tale there is the possibility of Love, symbolized by the lovely princess or the maiden in distress. She is the potential of the Feminine. She is the untouched ocean of My Love. Then there is the handsome prince who must go forth to rescue her. He represents the Will, Thought, the Divine Masculine. He is the bolt of lightning that is the stirring of Thought upon the Love that is My substance. This prince or hero must go forth to defeat the foe, be it dragon or sorcerer or even wicked little dwarfs. This is the *ego*, the world of illusion, the things that would keep destiny from being complete. The prince is successful.

He fights the dragon and rescues the princess, and with the kiss they are joined in Love, in bliss and . . . (what the fairy tales don't tell you) in Sacred Sexual union.

"This is where we are today. Those of you who are the leaders of this awakening, those of you who are hearing this voice, understanding these words, you have recognized the truth of your SoulMate. You have made the call. You may still have a few dragons to slay . . . but your true Love is on his or her way.

"Now, dear ones, comes the glorious truth. We have spoken of some of the gifts of this great union, of the generation of Love, of the womb of Creation. These things are important. They will serve you well until you can make The Shift. But, dear ones, I want to truly unveil something. I want to unveil to you the deepest truth of Sacred Sexuality. *Once revealed, there is no turning back.* Are you ready? Do not worry. For anyone not ready, this will make no sense, but if you are on the path of SoulMate Love, I promise this will *always* stay with you. And one day, when you lay your hand upon your beloved's chest and you feel the beating of his or her heart, you will know. You will remember that you are the center of Creation, that *you* are the stars, the Earth, the Moon. You will call forth the Love from in you that will *rend* the veil, that will melt the clouds of illusion. In that moment The Shift will occur, that Shift I have already spoken of when the background and the foreground switch. Then you will be Home.

"I tell you that all the heaven worlds, all the 'densities,' all the layers and the ladders and the hierarchies, are all your creation. *You do not need to come to Me in steps.* You do not need to 'go to Heaven' when you leave this world. You are only doing this because you can't imagine anything bigger! For surely if you think of it, if I am *everything*, then Heaven is not going to be like Earth.

"*Heaven is going to be the whirlwind of indescribable ecstasy in which you paint the glory of your beings across all Creation as you are joined in holy LoveMaking with your SoulMate.* Heaven is stars and worlds, galaxies and an indescribable kaleidoscope of life pouring forth before you, as your joined hearts are illuminated by your consciousness and given substance by your Love. And this, dear ones, is Sacred Sexuality. *This is the union of SoulMates!*

"Now you have a bit of the vision of the scope of who you are. You have a little taste of the worlds of Love you will create. *Now I will show you how you get there from here.*

"Today you are living in the physical world on a planet quickly becoming depleted in a time frame that most of you recognize *as the end of sustainable life on this world.* If you were to look at the truth (much of which is being hidden), you would see that truly the horrible depletion of resources and the increase in population, you do not have that many years. You are living in a world overcome with ego. Selfishness. Limitation. Terrible lack of vision. Pain. Disillusionment. The loss of marriage as a true spiritual contract. The loss of spirit as the center of human life.

"Into this scene I now come, telling you of glorious tomorrows, almost in the same sentence in which I tell you this world cannot long sustain you! How will you accomplish this? *Through Love.* And once you have this Love, how will you know how to make this mighty shift? *Through Sacred Sexuality.*

"Time is an illusion. Those of you reading this most likely understand. But what you don't understand is this: *the moment of Creation is still happening.* Dear ones, it is in progress this very minute. *The 'Big Bang' is exploding right now.* The lightning bolt of my longing for you, the rushing wind of My need to give forth My Love, the awakening of that need and that Love into a glorious explosion of ecstasy—*it is happening right now.*

"On every level. In every being. In every degree of motion. *The explosion of this Love as the great LoveMaking pours forth as life in ecstasy every moment through all eternity,* an ecstasy of such joy that you cannot even conceive of it. It is a union of such passion that the *very heart of God is opened to encompass all of Creation in this moment of magnificence!* Open to acknowledge the glorious, fiery, joy of Love. *That heart is you.*

"It is you who are opened to encompass everything! Let Me repeat this sentence. It is you who are opened in glorious ecstasy! Opened to encompass all of Creation in Love. *This is who you really are!* Now here you are on Earth, this little theater of struggle and limitation, and this is what you *think* you are. This what you are *pretending* to be, for reasons we

have already discussed.

"Creation is happening NOW. This amazing, glorious explosion of Love (shall we be graphic? The most amazing climax to LoveMaking you have ever experienced in any of your many lives, multiplied times not one billion, multiplied by ten billion) is happening every moment, creating the most indescribable joy and ecstasy.

"When you came forth to create yourselves as independent co-creators, *you took this experience of ecstasy with you.* You took it with you because it is who you are. You also took it with you so you would never forget the truth of your nature. Then you moved 'away from Me' *in your belief.* For dear ones, *our belief is all there is. You could not 'go' anywhere! Everything is us!*

So you chose to turn your consciousness *away from Me* and from the continual experiencing of our grand truth. Of course this worked because you can create anything you want.

"When you first turned your beloved consciousness 'away' (or 'down' the vibrational scale), you were in constant LoveMaking. You knew the truth of who you were. You were of course in union with your SoulMate. As you danced and swirled and flew through Creation, the 'sparks of your Love' flew everywhere, creating worlds and solar systems and anything you would imagine. Since you were locked in your SoulMate embrace in continual explosion of ecstasy, everything you brought into consciousness, you created.

"As you traveled, all that was

being created by Me and by you was inside of you. This means the glory of My LoveMaking, the literal creation of Love in the union of the two parts of My being was created as you moved.

"*Remember, you are my heart,* encompassing all of Creation. My heart wide open in the ecstasy of a grand sexual union (your best experience times ten billion!) This energy was joined with My consciousness and thus new and magnificent creations were 'spewing forth' in great explosions of Love. Add this to the two of you, who are the cells of My heart, joined in glorious SoulMate union, 'spewing forth' creations (everything you thought of while Making Love came into being, and you were Making Love continually.)

"*Well, all of these creations,*

Mine and yours, were manifesting as My Love ignited into form through consciousness. And since you were My heart, all these things created were created in you. (Trust Me on this.)

"Now, as you flew, danced and exploded in Love, *you became fascinated by all these new creations manifesting within you!* You could not help yourselves. You turned and looked within. And you were fascinated by what you saw— *and that is how you got here, where you are today.*

"I have described this as a theater with all of the SoulMate couples peering down in, as if it were a stage for marionettes. Yet it is not marionettes you are looking at. It is versions of you, your creations fueled by My explosions of energy and brought forth into 'form' by the power of your consciousness.

"So, for all this time the 'larger you' has been peering down in, totally absorbed by what you see ('smaller' versions of you). The more absorbed you got, the more fascinated with the show, *the less LoveMaking you were doing.* So you became more dense, since your attention was turned away from Me. You were cooling off as I so aptly expressed it another time because you were not generating the heat of passion and ecstasy. Thus, you got 'cooler and cooler' and then your creations became almost immovable because the Love of which they are made got 'too cold.' They were moving too slowly, cut off from the heat of LoveMaking.

"This, dear ones, is why I speak

of the perceptual shift. You must turn around. You must somehow 'tear yourselves away' from the theater, the illusion, which has you mesmerized. When you do, when you turn back around, you will see the truth! You will see the huge cosmos of which you are a part! You will see all of the beings that occupy this great cosmos with you. *You will see Me, and you will remember who you are.* Then you will be free, completely free! Free to rejoin Me in the truth of my heart. Free to be in continual glorious ecstatic LoveMaking with your SoulMate. Free to be co-creators. Free, dear ones, to understand that you are in existence as a universal being together with your SoulMate, and free to understand that you, humanity, make up My Heart! *Think upon this deeply.* It is very important.

"So—this is where we are. You are still peering intently into yourselves, watching all the characters you have created from yourselves! They are far enough from the warming Love; the continual explosion and they *move so slowly* that something called Time has come to exist. You are stuck, dear ones, stuck looking into the theater of yourselves *as you keep getting cooler inside because you are turned away from Me.*

"I can't risk losing you forever. I can't allow you to freeze. <u>So I have sent forth a call. I have made a decree.</u> Because you are still a part of Me, *you have to respond. For in essence, I am asking this of My own heart.* If I am determined, then My heart must obey. So I have decreed that all that is turned away from Me must now return, must turn around to face Me, to see Me. In doing so, the warmth of My Love will 'thaw' your insides and you will be able to return to your great cosmic LoveMaking. All will be well. This is what we are calling My 'In-breath.'

"How on Earth (or in Heaven!) do I get you to turn around? For being co-creators, of course you have Free Will. Here's how. Since all of Creation is within Me, when I send forth My decree, every particle of Creation will respond. For it's all part of Me. So the heart cells of the 'characters in the theater' *will begin to come back.*

"These are parts of *you*, My beloved ones, all the way down here in the theater or the dream. And when you 'rend the veil' (when **you** change your reality), you will recognize yourselves and then 'snap out of it.' You will turn away from the dream to be amazed and completely lifted in gratitude for the beauty you see as the truth of who you are.

"Now here is how you do this, My beloved children. Though you seem so far away, lost in layer upon layer of created 'realities,' you are very close to this awakening, *for My attention is now turned to you. Do you realize what this means? It means that great rays of My Love are pouring to you, penetrating the illusion, pouring through you.* So that all you have to do is 'catch' one of these rays of truth and you will be lifted immediately. It means that the truth of Creation is right here, 'between the cracks' in your reality. And what is the truth of Creation? It is the explosion of ecstasy that is continually and eternally happening. The truth is glorious cosmic LoveMaking where the thought of My giving sparks the ocean of My Love. The 'Big Bang.'

"Since Time is an illusion, the result of your 'freezing' in matter, if you can heat yourselves up enough to 'flow again,' you will move beyond Time. You will come in contact with the great ecstatic explosion of Creation and you will be free. Home.

"You will be expanding in the glorious recognition of the truth of your SoulMate and the amazing experience that SoulMate means. *You will be free*, free to be forever in glorious union with your SoulMate in the passion and ecstasy that are your heritage as My heart. Free to dance across Creation, spreading your consciousness and wrapping all thoughts you share in Love to bring them forth. Your 'children' will then be universes born of the seed of creative thought within the womb of Love. Free. Not to 'ascend' through the upward levels of reality. Not free to be in Heaven. No. *Free to be the heart of All That Is.*

"And how do you get there from here? Here, living on Earth in the middle of this dream? *By recreating the truth and following it Home. The truth is your union with your SoulMate in the glorious explosion of the Moment of Creation which is happening Now.* Always. In this now. And this now. And this now.

"First, of course, you must remember your SoulMate. You must clear away the illusion enough that you can be with them. You must call them forth by choosing to be in Love. Then, *once you have your SoulMate and you are in union consciously, you must break through the illusion of Time while Making Love, through the connection with your orgasm to the Now Moment of Creation which is the explosion of My Love into all that is.*

"And how do you do this? Through your cells. Actually, through the atoms at the heart of your cells. *For the explosion of Creation is the atomic substance of Love poured forth in great intensity and heat (friction of movement).*

"*The substance of your very being is made out of the substance of Creation,* formed in the Now moment in which I am ever bringing you forth into existence. Ah, dear ones, you speak often of cellular memory. You have no idea! *For within your cells, within the atoms of what you believe to be your physical body (and your physical world) is Creation happening now.* In the heart of each atom, in the dance of the electrons, *is* the experience of Creation coming forth into this 'form' shaped by your greater SoulMate consciousness.

"However difficult this is for you to comprehend (and for some it may be impossible), *if you trust this energy, it will take you Home.* In your very cells there is a pulsation of light that goes 'in and out' – in to the reality of the Creation of your original SoulMate selves and out to connect with the moment of Creation, the energy of the Great LoveMaking. *It is the 'atomic' energy that fuels life. Without it, nothing would be here.*

"*So, when you are making Love with your SoulMate, you can build up to this point, the point of riding your ecstasy, the climax of your LoveMaking, back out of Time and back to Me.* If you are conscious of your ability as co-creators as well, you can generate enough heat, enough energy, you can get your actual electrons moving so quickly that you will unfreeze the whole dream as you make the connection to the eternal Now. You can remember, remember and turn back to Me. Then instantly, every single cell of your heart will be returned to My reality, *the reality*, the only one that is eternal. For there are *many, many* creations, all of which seem like a reality when in truth, they are not.

   "*The ignition switch, the connecting 'electricity' or actual 'atomic power' is in your cells, dear ones.* However, what you know as atomic power is dangerous. Why?

Because it is atomic power at the lowest and slowest vibration of this most dense reality. It has cooled SO much that it can destroy the energy it is made of. Atomic energy at this level, this very most dense level of your lowest reality, is the 'reversal' or 'flip side' or mirror image of the true atomic energy. *It does have the potential to destroy the substance of Love, which is life.*

"So you must take the atomic reaction and go deeper still. Deeper to the heart of the atom. *In the heart of the atom you will find yourselves – you and your SoulMate.* At the 'smallest' end of the scale of your being, you are My heart. This means you exist on every level, in every dimension at every size. I have told you that *you can reach Me by going within or by going without* (meaning expanding into the largest thing).

"Dear ones, at this level where you are now —the you that is reading this message – there is no way you can get Home to Me through expansion. It is too far and takes too much energy. Since you have no concept here of the SIZE of Creation. I must ask again that you trust me on this.

"But though you cannot reach the original Creation, the 'Big Bang,' the explosion that I am by expansion, <u>you can reach it by going within,</u> by going inward to the very atoms of which you are made. The universe is a hologram. You can access the whole from the parts with far less energy than it takes to become the whole. Thus, you can go within. Within, within and deeper within, waking every cell into remembrance of the LoveMaking energy that I am.

"This is what each of you can experience, a deliberate waking of your body to the remembrance of My True nature. *You can learn to generate the atomic union which is the spiritual level of the atomic fusion of which atom bombs are made!* Just by sensing the power of the negative use of this energy, *you can sense the power of Creation living in your cells, activated with your SoulMate, joining you to the ever present, ongoing atomic explosion of Creation.*

"Just remember that on this level, it is atoms of the most incredible light, creating life, the explosion that created all universes in Me. *This is what you will connect to in the glory of your SoulMate LoveMaking. And then by your consciousness, as you explode in unison with Me as a cell of My heart, you will easily (so* _easily) lift the veil, freeing all humanity in one moment of fiery union._

"Trust Me to lead you, dear ones. For now, I have revealed to you the secrets of Creation. I have trusted you. I trust you now with the very keys to all the power in all the universes. All That Is. But to hear this you must listen with your heart. To open the door of Creation with the key, you must be with your SoulMate. And this is this information kept save. For those who might use it for destructive purposes do not know Love and not knowing Love, they do not have their SoulMate.

"Without their SoulMate, they could be standing in the midst of all their Power, of everything I am in Love and thought, and _they could do nothing. This is why Creation_ *has ever been safe from the destructiveness of mankind because only Love can take you out of the 'safe place' of Time and Space and limitation.* Only a true elevated heart can find Love. Thus, has this world existed for so many years as the 'incubation chamber' of humanity, a place where human beings can hurt themselves but can never touch the rest of Creation.

"Say 'Yes,' dear ones! Say 'Yes' to Love. Read these words and let them decode themselves in your joined hearts. Say 'Yes' to Love and reach for Me, and I can promise you that these messages that hold the keys will be revealed to you, to your full understanding."

As you see from the Message, "The Atomic Power of SoulMate Love and the Keys to Using It," the power of our sexuality is an amazing and beyond important topic for us to understand. If you feel overwhelmed from reading that

Message, please remember that God has informed us that Twin Flame Love will be our study in the years that stretch before us. We can only imagine that there will be more Messages and personal communications, guiding and leading us slowly and patiently, with the deep Love of God for His/Her children.

In the meantime, know that the whole second half of the volume, "Say YES to Love, God Unveils SoulMate Love and Sacred Sexuality" is given to different aspects of sexuality, including discussion of our current ways of viewing it. (SP)

GOD SPEAKS:

"The pure essence of creative power is sexual. Thus, sexual union with Love will empower humanity and all that is within them. Such reclamation of sexual union with an open heart will, of course, begin to draw SoulMates quickly back into conscious reunion. This done, humanity will be returned to its true lineage – the great 'explosion of light' that is the continual union of SoulMates on the higher levels.

Life will open up.

"In every cell you know this truth, and the fact that you are separated in Consciousness is the source of all human loneliness. This beautiful communion is what is ahead of you. Now, as the veil is lifted, it is critical that this awareness be returned to humanity. In this union is your true creative power, and in your creative power lies the healing of the world. How quickly this happens and how easily depends on the number of people who can say 'yes' to their SoulMate, thus reclaiming the great creative power of their Sacred Sexuality, and thus raising up all the being of Love of which you are made, My beloved children.

". . . the simple message of the truth of Love (opening the heart), the assurance of the returning awareness of your SoulMates (for of course they are always there) and the recognition of the great, joyous power for good that is human sexuality will be recognized by all. It will be recognized because it is time. It is the key to the homecoming. *If even a few receive the information at first, those few can completely elevate the whole of humanity.*

"Please! Do everything you can to understand the truth of this. Please read these words. Please open your hearts. Please trust in the truth of Love. And please vow, with the great power and gifts that are yours, to serve the awakening of all humanity. The truth of who you are means this. <u>It will take very few awakened SoulMates, relative to the whole of</u> humanity, to set in motion the revolution of Love that

<u>will awaken everyone</u>. It will take very few SoulMate couples, who know the truth of who they are, to get the blood pumping fully, in a glory of life and awakening, through all of My heart—meaning all of humanity. The truth of Love will spread quickly. The giving of Love will nourish everything."

PART THREE :

PRA, SHANNA'S TWIN

FLAME, ANSWERS

YOUR QUESTIONS

In this part of the book, Pra, Shanna's Twin Flame, answers questions that people have asked us about Twin Flames. As noted earlier, Pra is not in an embodiment on Earth at this time, but rather, resides in consciousness. For this reason, he is free of many of the limitations in perspective that life in a vehicle on the Earth creates. [1]

* * *

Question #1: I have a question that I would like to ask Pra that isn't directly about Twin Flames but is more about our life on Earth. We have been told that you, Pra, are not on the Earth plane, not in a physical body. And so, we know that this means that you are not subject to the duality and the often-selfish games of the ego on Earth. We have been told that you are in a place where you are able to maintain your vibration at the level of Only Love and see truthfully.

Here on Earth, we can easily become confused as to who we are and what we are doing here. Can you give us some insights about who we really are that might help us to live a more meaningful life here?

PRA: This is a huge and most wonderful question. There IS great confusion and misunderstanding among beings on Earth as to who you are. That is why we have been directed to write this book.

First and foremost, we are all Divine Beings— you, me and everyone on Earth, and everyone on every other plane of existence. We are all ONE with God, our Source; ONE with Love, ONE with each other.

God is infinite. In our Oneness with God, each of us is one of the infinite forms of the one God, the one Consciousness, the one Love, the one Light. God lives through each one of us and pours out a unique expression of Love and goodness: AS us, IN us and THROUGH us.

You are here on Earth in forms (bodies), but these forms are not who you are. You are a divine essence. The forms may change at any time, but your essence is eternal. For every being on Earth, no matter how you are expressing in this Earth life, it is most important to understand your true identity. Your true identity is: you are an expression of the One God, a being of Love and Light, with all of the divine qualities. And of course, at this moment, you are living all of this through a physical vehicle.

Many on Earth get confused and make their physical life, its circumstances, or even their physical characteristics their identity.

They do this unknowingly, innocently. These

vehicles are just the FORMS through which you are expressing. THESE ARE NOT THE ESSENCE OF WHO YOU ARE.

There is the symbol of the ocean. The ocean is our Oneness with God. You can take a cup of water out of the ocean. You can pour it out, and you can see drops of water. But you can't take drops of water away and have them exist separately. The drops of water might represent each individual unique expression, but they are still all connected to the whole. You can't separate them.

There's another important awareness about which I wish to speak. Earthlings need to clear out any doubt in anyone's mind that God is anything but pure Love and goodness. If there is any confusion in any being about God—anything disharmonious or problematical in one's mind on this subject. That needs to be cleared to experience the fullness of Love that we really are and that is present. What if someone is harboring doubts about God's purity or Love or goodness. This is not truth and needs to be cleared away. Problems and disharmonious situations are not who we are. They are simply places to clear to see the Love that is there.

Let me explain. People's experiences in the world are imbued with the duality that is present here on Earth. There is always an opposite for anything you experience here. For example, you say, "I had a good day," or "I had a bad day." Thinking in duality, a person may make a judgment about things they see in the world around them: pain, suffering, starvation and so on. There is confused thinking that duality (good and bad) and distortions seen in life on Earth might be part of God. There is also judgment about God for allowing such things to occur.

These are not truth. God is nothing but pure Love and goodness, and that is also the truth of who you are.

There is nothing else in you, no matter what is appearing before your eyes in the current distortions of life on Earth.

So each of your expressions, however you uniquely express, is pure Love and goodness. This is the truth of each person and why each of you is here—to pour out Love and goodness, creatively, uniquely. Each being is an expression of Oneness with God, here on this plane and on any other plane on which you might reside.

The Twin Flame relationship reflects this all-encompassing union and the Love and goodness and is an important way of giving and receiving Love, fully and purely. We see the longing on the Earth of people to love one's partner, the person that is right for them in relationship, one's Twin Flame. There is a longing here for that—to love

and to receive the love from one's Twin Flame,
that comfort and understanding as an expression
of God's Love. This Love is one's true identity
and it is meant to be expressed and experienced.
People have the longing, and they know that
there has to be someone out there who is the
perfect partner for them.

When you acknowledge this, it will ignite the
Twin Flame.

The desire will open it. The longing that you
have to give and receive from the Twin Flame is
the expression of God's Love. It is meant to be
expressed through the physical body. I am
validating here the truth of your longing.

Dear ones, all of you—including my beloved,
Shanna—many of you signed up to come here
because assistance was needed on Earth, and you
answered the call to help. Humanity has gotten
confused. There is often not clarity here at this
time as to the truth. The truth, I repeat, is that
God is nothing but pure Love and goodness and
that is also the truth of who you are. This
confusion as to what is the truth is why many of
you who are on Earth in your physical bodies are
experiencing right now what I call "foggy
energies" that are covering the truth. Behind the
clouds is the sun; behind the turbulent energies
is the Love. The fog is everything that is not the
truth that I have just clarified for you—the Love

and goodness of God. You have been living lives in duality and confusion, and you are now clearing all the distorted experiences, emotions and thoughts, returning these to the Oneness, with Love, knowing yourself as the Oneness of Love. The Twin Flame relationship clearly shows the truth of this.

Question #2: My question for Pra is can you give us some guidance as to how to begin to open up to the Twin Flame.

PRA: I am happy to speak about this and I don't think my answer will surprise you. The best place to begin is where and how you are feeling Love, right now in your life.

What in your life is opening the spark of Love for you? Wherever you feel the spark of Love is where to begin building more Love and your focus on the Twin Flame.
You may be someone who is already focusing your Love on God or focusing your Love on your Twin Flame. But if you are not aware of your Twin, this Love in your life can be focused on animals, a child, a romantic partner, nature, art, anything in which you feel your heart open and you feel the Love clearly.

Then, give yourself permission to explore that area, whatever it is. As you stay open, and continue with the area where you feel Love, before you know it, suggestions of the Twin Flame will begin to appear. Love is what draws the Twin. Your life will begin to take on a wonderful amazing quality of aliveness and richness which will open everything up. So, begin where the feeling is strong and let it build and show you the Love you are!

Question #3: My question is how can I keep my little mind and its judgments from interfering with my desire to stay open to my Twin Flame?

PRA: Remember, the Twin Flame is always ONE—one with you, one with God. Whether the Twin Flame partner appears in a body or in some other form. whether complete, as it is at the Moment of Creation, or fragmenting itself in a journey through the universe, the Twin Flame is always connected with the partner on all levels. ALWAYS. Even when you cannot perceive this at all, it is still a truth.

You asked about judgments of the little mind. It doesn't matter how you see the identity of the Twin Flame on the Earth plane. The Twin can be in any life situation, whatsoever. Their true identity is not what they are living here. The seeming life situation on Earth is not important. *What is important is the Love.* The Twin is always there with you. The Twin is also always overseeing his or her other half, always assisting to open the heart of his or her Twin and to assist to connect with one's true essence, always reaching for the highest vibration and connection to God.

Often, we are caught in our own issues and the confusion does not allow us to see the Twin. The Twin Flame always sees its partner in his or her perfection, in their energy signature. The Twin lives in the fullness of Love at all levels, so that when you wish to open to the Twin, the essence of your Twin is always available. When awareness does occur, it can clear the energy. It will be resonating with your full, unencumbered self.

Now here is an important point. It's IMPORTANT to be purely yourself. Embrace the truth of your unique expression, as the divine feminine or masculine you are. Listen to what is right for you and follow through on what brings joy, and this is how one embodies the energy frequency that matches you with your Twin.

Focus on the Love, the Love of God, the energy of one's own being. All of this is the energy of Oneness and helps to draw the Twin. Be willing and open. Release preconceived ideas of how you think your Twin should look on the Earth. Simply let the Twin show up and reveal himself or herself to you. Take steps to deepen your relationship with God, and with LOVE. The Creator experiences itself as the Love you are being as a Twin Flame couple.

Question #4: Pra, can you please clarify for us how we might recognize our Twin Flame?

PRA: Dear ones, what I see from my perspective is that people here on Earth are coming more and more rapidly toward this concept of the Twin Flame, but some of them are still saying, "Huh?"

Dear ones, there is no way to fully explain the two who are Twin Flames—great souls. This is not the same as dating, as looking for a physical plane partner, as looking for a husband or wife.

Once you become aware of this connection with your Twin, once you understand the essence of the Twin Flame, the two of you—the truth will pour through every one of your many incarnations, your memories, and every one of the beings so involved will realize the truth of who they really are and call forth the connection. As a person focuses on the Love, living and being that Love for the good of all, feeling the Oneness with all, this lifts and opens their energy, and they see and experience their Twin more clearly. The experiences people have with their Twin is often so incredible, so ecstatic and blissful beyond what people usually experience on the Earth.

Please listen. To understand this, I ask that you open your heart and open your mind. I guarantee that in every incarnation, every person you have ever been with was your Twin Flame—reflecting to you the state of consciousness of your awareness at that time, be it open or be it dim. The reason for this is because we are One, with God, with Spirit, with consciousness itself. That Oneness is always present.

When a being is in a relationship and I mean each and every relationship, the person's Twin Flame is present there too, equally. There may not be awareness of this, but the two are always reflecting the Love back and forth to one another. That Love is the draw toward the Love—no matter how much awareness of the Twin Flame one has. Whether the person has awareness of the concept of the Twin Flame or not, they still have the draw toward Love, toward the reflection of the Twin Flame that one is, drawing back and forth to one another.

To the degree that one is open to one's relationship with God, that is the degree to which you will encounter someone who is able to reflect it back. All will experience this kind of feedback. You will experience the feedback of the

Love and/or you will experience the feedback of the seeming separation. If one of the Twin Flames is awakening, he or she can help the other to wake up, to increase the awareness.

Question #5: My dearest Pra, Shanna here. I would like to pose a question using my own life as an example so that the idea of the Twin Flame being present in every person with whom you have ever interacted may be clear to all of us. I am referring to what you spoke about earlier— that every person with whom you have ever had a relationship, a connection, an adventure is reflecting a "piece of your Twin Flame."

One of my partners from the past was a man to whom I was drawn early in my life because he seemed to me to be very secure in his life circumstances. At that time, I was very insecure, and this made him attractive to me. Pra, you are saying he was reflecting you, my Twin Flame, without me realizing it?

PRA: It seemed to you that he brought you a quality—security—that really only happens with God. Your security is only in God. The draw toward security is really a reflection of the draw toward God's Love. What you, Shanna, were being drawn toward during that relationship, even if you weren't consciously aware of it, was

love of God in the form of the experience of
security.

In our oneness with God that is also oneness
with one's Twin, we are not lacking anything. We
are always secure. Love always provides
everything needed, including a physical body on
this earth. This provision is a form of Love that
can be translated into the word "secure."

Even if at that time, you, Shanna, knew
nothing of the concept of the Twin Flame, or even
if many personality factors were operating
underneath it, the truth is that my Love, Pra's
Love (your Twin Flame) was coming through,
providing security. The Twin will come through
in different ways, showing the deeper truth, even
if the person doesn't realize that the Twin is
present.

Relationships are meant to be an experience of
Love. Love is always there, no matter how little,
or what form it takes, whether it is there with or
without awareness. Yet, the truth of this and
every relationship is that you both had an
intrinsic draw to God, no matter how large or
small the level, and whether you had any
realization of it or not.

God is always calling us. This intrinsic call is
to be in relationship, even if it is just for security.
Whatever draw is calling us to relationship, it is
God on some level. Love is always present, even

if the level of awareness doesn't appear to us that way.

Everyone has a strong draw for love no matter what the circumstances are.

With any form of relationship in which a person finds themselves, it is some form of Love that wants to be expressed. Each one will have different qualities, but it is some form of Love. The Twin Flame relationship reflects back to each other that everyone is the whole. They have all the divine qualities. They aren't missing anything.

Question #6: Did we not fragment ourselves after the Moment of Creation, as we travelled through Creation? We have read about this in different sources. Are there not portions of us floating around that we left behind in our travels? Perhaps these are portions that are seemingly separate from the whole of us that we need to draw back to us, that we need to integrate into our whole?

PRA: Well, now I must bring awareness to the problems that sometimes arise with language. This could be a way to put it into English language to attempt to explain this concept. BUT "fragment" is not meant to be looked upon as a mistake. Or even less than or portioned off from the whole. A fragment, as it is used in this context, is not meant to be considered limiting at all.

When a being is in human form, that person has a purpose unique to the human form. Each way we appear, whatever it is, has a unique purpose. Those who are here on this Earth or in any other place where we might be for the purpose of serving the expression of Love of the One—that is not a fragment in the sense of "less than" or limiting one's abilities. Each level has a specific purpose of the expression of Love. It is always about Loving.

And, I understand what you are asking. All of those are just the places in consciousness—as on the Earth—where beings have experienced forgetfulness and lost awareness of who they truly are. They think they are lacking and limited. They really aren't. Those ideas are the places in consciousness that the being needs to open to his or her fullness again, to remember that they are One. The forgetting that you imagine you experienced—it's not really the truth. We are all whole and complete with the Moment of Creation, remembering who we are. Everyone who is on the Earth is the wholeness of all, as I have explained—not separate or apart.

Question #7: How many sparks of Light were

there at the Moment of Creation that might have gone on to become Twin Flames or right now who are in bodies on Earth?

PRA: There is no number. It is an infinity, an infinity of Love. God is always an infinity. Twin Flames that come together expand the Love more and more and more. Understand—we have never really left parts of ourselves. It is only in our thinking. Our focus rests on certain parts, and then we forget some of the other parts. We forget the seeming parts of us that we are using or forget what we are not using in the present moment, what we are not aware of or what we are not focusing on. No matter where or when one is on the spectrum of Creation, everyone is always One with the whole.

Question #8: Is it true that there is no one on the Earth in a body who does not have the potential of connecting with his or her TwinFlame?

PRA: That is correct. People are one with their Twin in an energy sense wherever they are, even if they don't see it. People get focused on what seems to be one piece, one part of the whole. But they are always the wholeness. This is just a temporary confusion. They are never separate from it. With their Twin, they are the wholeness without question or doubt. As Twin Flames come together again on Earth, as they were created at the Moment of Creation, this will continue to bring a greater awareness of what we are talking about. But every person has the potential to connect at the level of the Twin.

Question #9: What about people who don't seem to have any interest in a relationship or in exploring the possibility of the Twin Flame? What if they read this book, but they don't seem called at all to explore this? Or may even doubt that it is happening at all.

PRA: There is nothing right or wrong about this. However, people who are avoiding relationship may be missing the opportunity to know more of themselves and to know more of the natural progression of Love.

Some people are focusing only on God. If they are holding everyone else out of the possibility of that relationship, that is another way of looking at the seeming illusion of separation. The truth is God is in and out of everything—animals, nature, and so on—and the Twin Flame relationship is a reflection of that. The key is not to separate yourself in any way from the expression of relationship of Love that comes through our connection with all these various forms, all these relationships.

Some people may be holding off because of experiences of having been hurt in relationships. These are places where they are still holding the illusion of separation. They have the opportunity to resolve this. If they resolve it, they become open to all kinds of relationships. They are open then to the explosion of Love that is in every form and every relationship. This can include relationship with a work buddy, a brother, sister, teacher, and so on. The Twin Flame relationship can encompass every kind of relationship one could have.

Question # 10: So what is most important for one of us to hold in my mind while desiring to make contact with the Twin Flame, in embodiment or otherwise?

PRA: What is most important is to stay open to an ever-higher type of Love. Anyone may come up against a temporary block in a relationship. What I mean by block in this case is the feeling of wanting to have a higher flow of Love, a greater flow of Love that can be reciprocated more and more and more. The Twin is always hovering there wanting to encourage his or her partner. Any place the person becomes open, the

Love will come through. The Moment of Creation represents the fullness of Love that is present all the time to the degree that we are open to be able to experience it. It is happening all the time, but we cannot experience it until we are willing to open. Reach higher.

Question #11: What if I meet a person to whom I am drawn, and that person is unavailable? What if the person is married or in another serious relationship?

PRA: It is very possible for someone to see glimpses of the Twin Flame coming through someone who is in another relationship and so is unavailable. It can get confusing. A person might experience a heart opening with a certain person. They can even recognize the love of their Twin in this experience. It is a true energy experience. The life circumstances will show if this is going to be a realized in the physical Twin Flame experience or remain as just a heart opening that is not intended to be realized in bodies.

If there is no reciprocal energy, they need to let the possibility of relationship go. The life circumstances will show whether this is to be a "lived out" Twin Flame relationship on this dimension or whether it was simply meant to be a beautiful heart opening.

People get attached to the form where they experienced the heart opening and the feeling of Love. But this is not about attachment to form, and this can cause confusion. One can think they have to have the form that was the cause of the heart opening. When there is an attachment like that, there is a piece of something they are looking for—the essence or the divine flavor of Love that they think can only come through that person. The truth is LOVE IS EVERYWHERE. We are never separate from it. IT IS NOT TRUTH THAT LOVE ONLY COMES THROUGH ONE PARTICULAR FORM.

In these cases, if the person were able to let go of the attachment to form, and return to the focus on Love of God, and Love itself and continue asking for the Love of the Twin, the Love could take on another form that would be available and appropriate to hold the Love of the Twin for that person.

Question # 12: I am very attracted to someone, and he or she is a famous person who is not readily accessible to me—not available to me. I feel strongly that this person is my Twin Flame. Do I give up? What if I feel some level of Love but I am not sure how to proceed? Do I try to make contact?

PRA: The answer to this question is similar to the previous question. The truth is that this has been an experience with the Twin Flame to open the heart, but this is not the vehicle the Twin Flame is to come through on a long-term basis, unless there is some clear indication—mutual response, a circumstance or situation where the two could continue to explore the relationship. There would be a willingness of both people, and the circumstances would provide opportunities for them to be together.

You can understand that this is the same situation when a person has a Twin Flame experience with someone who is clearly unavailable. The person who had the original Twin Flame contact may want to hold on because they are afraid of losing that incredible feeling of Love. However, the person needs to focus on the Love again. It will be stronger and clearer because of this experience.

If they will stay with the Love and release the fear of losing Love, the feeling will come again in another vehicle. Giving and giving and giving Love keeps them in the experience of Love. It would be good to detach from this unavailable person who was a subject of the original experience and focus on the feeling of Love.

Question #13: Is there any way to know when or

where my Twin Flame will appear?

PRA: Although loving one's Twin opens the heart and energy to experience the Twin, the personality self on the Earth plane cannot control the time or place or circumstances of profound Twin Flame experiences. This is the reason that people often become focused or fixated on one person in a vehicle. Sometimes one has an experience of their Twin so profound that they cannot control what is happening. It is an incredible heart opening and they want to validate it by creating a permanent relationship with the being who was the cause of it. They are afraid they will not have it with another person.

I am letting you know that these profound experiences can happen. We cannot control when it will happen, but when you keep going into the Love, you will have more experiences beyond this initial one. There is no way to anticipate ahead of time what the next experience will look like. LOVE IS ALWAYS OPENING MORE. AND MORE. AND MORE. THERE IS NO SUCH THING AS LOSS OF LOVE.

Keep focusing on giving love. Continually. Morning, noon and night. All the time!

Question #14: What if I am with someone, someone I have been with a long time and someone I love and respect? I don't want to give up this person and go searching for my Twin Flame. How can my Twin Flame come through the person I am with?

PRA: I would like to use my beloved Shanna as an example in explaining this. In order to do the Twin Flame work that Shanna and I agreed to do during this, our present assignment for God, together we agreed that it was in the highest good for her to be in physical form and for me to be in consciousness. She, therefore, agreed to be without a long-term Earth partner.

When Shanna met Joseph, they recognized each other as beings who had known and respected each other before. They felt drawn to be together in physical form to fulfill desires for companionship and support each other in their spiritual work. The Twin Flame delights in every opportunity his or her Twin might have for joy and fulfillment. There are no conflicts. I, Pra, felt it was very important for my beloved Shanna to have the Love and the physical plane experience with someone like Joseph who is equally devoted to Love and to God and to serving humanity as well.

It was clear that this would be a relationship with dedication to loving God, and that every part of the life they would share would be spiritually focused. I as Shanna's Twin Flame could come through easily and match the energy signature that she had with Joseph because he had such an open heart. If your partner has an open heart, it makes the Twin Flame very accessible.

So the answer to the question, "how can I connect with my Twin Flame if I am with this other person" is: every time both hearts are open, the Twin Flame is right there in the midst of the Love that is being shared and expressed. The existing relationship can be the vehicle for them to have an experience of the Love in a physical form that they are having with the Twin Flame on other non-physical levels at the same time, but they may not be conscious of this because attention is focused on the physical.

Question #15: So, how can I be more aware of my Twin Flame even though I don't want to leave my present partner?

PRA: As you continue to open to the love in any form, you will become more aware of your Twin Flame. It is a matter of going more deeply into Love as you open your energy more and more. You become more aware. Also as you do your own clearing work, clearing the places where you have blocks and are still holding the idea of seeming separation, the love opens up. You become completely transparent. Completely open. You can then be more aware of your Twin Flame, just by loving. The loving must be unconditional. When things arise, keep things clear. Unconditional Love doesn't confuse things that arise as blocking the truth or holding judgments against themselves or the person with whom they are in relationship. Unconditional love knows the true identity of the person.

Question #16: Can you be in touch with your Twin Flame when you are going through challenges? Can they help? Shanna mentioned that she was less able to be aware of you when she was experiencing her Dark Night of the Soul.

PRA: Even if you are not able to be directly conscious of your Twin in such a situation, your Twin can help by coming through another person. The Twin is always desirous of helping, if help is needed. In Shanna's case, Joseph happened to be part of her spiritual group. He was a beautiful heart whom she "knew" from other incarnations. I as her Twin was able to utilize Joseph to do many things for her and to speak to her in encouraging ways when that was what she needed.

She was vibrationally closer to Joseph than

she was to me in the higher dimensions. He was easier for her to reach at that moment. She felt a heart that was open. My heart, Pra, her Twin Flame, was sending energy to her through Joseph, and a familiar feeling reached her. Both Joseph and I were being the open heart, and it gave her the possibility of experiencing the Shanna/Pra Twin Flame energy signature without impediment. Though she was herself in a lower vibration experience, the power of my heart allowed her to go through the doorway and open to a higher vibration. Joseph, because of his compassion and openheartedness, offered that beautiful gift at that moment.

It could also be a Master or Guide or Angel who could be utilized by the Twin when a message is needed to be delivered or support is needed. The Twin is always aware of such moments and is looking for an appropriate avenue of contact.

Question #17: Pra, I definitely want to have the experience of reconnecting with my Twin Flame, either in meditation the way Shanna and you did it or with a person who comes into my life who can reflect that to me. If we are not yet physically with our Twin Flame, either because they are not on the Earth plane or because we haven't met them yet, how can we best connect with them to fulfill our divine mission?

PRA: Thank you for your dedication and determination. It will serve you well. I repeat again, the most important thing is to focus on Love. The focus on God, the focus on Love, and more specifically calling the Twin Flame to yourself is essential. Your energy, your Love is the vibrational signature that you are sending out. You may not recognize it initially, but you will. When you call to your Twin Flame, you are calling to your own specific signature—your vibrational resonance. It will feel so comfortable. So familiar. Do you remember in Shanna's story about our early meetings, she said that though at first she wasn't sure who I was, she felt as though she had known me all her life?

Then when you continue to send out the resonance, the Twin Flame will begin reflecting it back. It becomes a gradual and greater and greater felt sense experience.

The Twin Flame is a universal energy signature, the signature of God, the One, but you feel it not just on the universal. As you focus deeper and deeper and focus on the Love, you get the real feeling, the uniqueness of each Twin Flame signature. Now if there are judgments and qualities from third dimensional life about which you have prejudice, the ego is going to begin judging and you will lose that feeling. It completely depends on how much we can keep our hearts open. If you have some quality that you feel your Twin must match up to, the ego will create the mind chatter and the preconceived ideas. That is why you have to stay strongly in the heart and give the Love the greatest importance. Then the Twin Flame can enter. Remember, it matters not the costume or condition of the Twin within the Earth realm.

In the beginning when you sense the heart feeling strongly, you may not know if this person is going to be your business partner, or just a friend, but if you stay in the Love, it will sort itself out. Love and God will clear it up. Just stay in your heart and have trust.

Question #18: Pra, our brother, how do you keep the Love alive in this dimension on Earth; how do you sustain the focus on the Love? As you know, the pull into daily life here is very strong and can distract us from our higher spiritual purpose.

PRA: If you are with someone, hold on to the Love by making Love the first focus, even through the moments, the conversations, whatever distractions the Earth life presents. Keep removing your attention from the illusion as needed. When you are giving a lot of Love to your partner (or friend, or sister), the Love heats up. Love given becomes amplified and makes it easier to continuing the giving of Love.

Acknowledge small acts of Love and kindness —thank you for doing the laundry; bring a little gift; whatever you know expresses Love. The heart will keep on opening. Gestures of Love will keep the Love going and make it easier to experience the subtle entrances of the Twin Flame. Turn what seems like something very everyday into an act of Love and gratitude. Any expansion of Love lifts above seeming separation and changes the vibration into giving and receiving. Express your gratitude for the cornucopia of abundance of the harvest of God's gifts.

PRA: *Pra is looking out over humanity from his vantage point.* People desire the purest Love, but they often think the truth of Love is mysterious and hard to find. This is not the case.

If they will stay in the Love, they will be given clarity about it. All you need to do is stay in the heart and give up judgment. "Love has your back." If you start slipping into judgment, you will know your mind has taken over, and you are losing the focus on Love.

Return to the focus on Love. Return to the

focus on God. Return to the focus on the Light, and Love will return. As you return to the Love that you are, the expressions of Love with your Twin will be fulfilling beyond anything you could have imagined! We say YES to Love! Please, say YES to Love, too!

SHANNA VISITS WITH PRA
IN SANTA FE
November 11, 2018

While we are within the vibration of my beloved Pra, I will share with you, the reader, a recent visit I experienced with my Pra so that you may touch within your heart the feeling of bliss, experience the upliftment and thrill of a tangible visit from one's Twin Flame, if such is in Spirit. It is by reaching for the highest Love we desire in our hearts, by creating it with our thoughts, in our imagination, in our longing for the experience of the highest Love of which we feel capable that we draw the Twin Flame directly to us.

Last night I was having a sleepless night, not unusual for me as I am sometimes not a good sleeper. I started holding in my mind the beautiful I AM Presence poster (from St. Germain) which some of you will recall. There is a "divine being" in grand spiritual explosion at the top of the poster, connected by a vertical column to an earth being below—a depiction of our higher self and its connection with our Earth presence. I was reveling in the beauty and energy of the I AM Presence, identifying with the burst of light that represents our God Self, high above our human Earth self below it.

Then I felt the waves of light orgasmic ecstasy which characterize a visit from Pra. You see, it is in those moments when we can lift ourselves to that high vision of who we truly are that the Twin appears more easily. Since I was resting in bed and had no competing earthly pursuit at the moment, I felt myself easily let go completely of the body. It seemed I was being held in a large undefined oval-shaped container of energy, floating within it. As I realized that a Pra visit was in progress, I became very excited. There followed waves of ecstatic bliss, and I was held in constant gentle motion, almost rocked like a baby. I wasn't aware of Pra as an Earth-style "body" in this particular visit, but rather, as the familiar feeling of an energy that was flooding me.

We had a wonderful telepathic conversation including many endearments and expressions of emotion, with some words aloud here and there. Then Pra chose a topic that showed he had been listening to me for a while. He said that *we here on Earth should not concern ourselves with the way in which various spiritual teachings are given to us.*

That particular evening a group of us had been discussing (and comparing) some of the different teachings to which we had been drawn. All of the teachings, whatever they are, are all moving all of us on the God path Home toward our beloved Creator, he explained. Different teachings appeal to different people at different times. As he telepathed this, I could feel a movement beginning, a slow but steady motion toward "Home," like the gentle current of a river. We were all seemingly on this path of motion toward our Mother-Father-God.

Then Pra reminded me of a lovely painting that hangs on the wall in my living room (a print of a famous Christian painting called The Rapture) in which everyone on Earth is being gently magnetized off the Earth into the sky toward a glorious sun burst/depiction of the God Force at the top of the painting. Beings in all segments of the painting are floating gently away from their Earth homes toward the Creator in the top center of the painting. Pra referred to this image a few different times during our conversation.

Next, I was made aware of the Milky Way, the real thing in the sky. There are no street lights in the little town of La Cienega where we live, and the stars in the sky and the Milky Way are often very clear. There it was! And we were suddenly part of it! We were in the night sky over my house in Santa Fe, New Mexico, floating along in the star filled night while Pra talked about how nothing was solid, and *everything* was gradually dissolving more and more into pure liquid energy and floating toward God, in the way that the Milky Way seems to float.

There were many of us, and all were part of a visible broad, white band of moving energies. Some were more "solid" than others, but all seemed to be gradually surrendering their "form" and dissolving and moving upward toward what would be the Home of the Creator. We were gently floating as though we were part of a river of milk flowing along, dissolving our individuality as we floated—headed to God.

There were feelings of bliss and surrender; there was no reason to think or work or strive or do anything but allow.

Pra continued, referring to all the political confusion on the Earth, especially in the United States at the present time, and the idea conveyed telepathically was that some people needed to experience strong events in order to realize that we are all ONE and we are all LOVE and we are all returning to the Creator of All, equally. The idea was just to allow these beings to be where and as they are. Despite and regardless of how things seem to appear on earth, it was clear that everything is becoming more fluid, dissolving, and it is all moving in one direction: Home to God. The mental and emotional understanding of these ideas was mixed with delicious sensations of ecstatic waves and complete calm, rightness, comfort and trust.

I stayed quite a while inside my comfy oval bubble, enjoying the light orgasmic waves and chatting with Pra about various topics. Then I remember feeling sleepy and after a couple of tries, I fell solidly asleep (this in itself was amazing). Later I realized that Pra was playing "Sand Man," and that *he* had put me to sleep. I slept deeply, awakening once to say a few words to Joseph who had awoken beside me ("Pra was here") . . . then falling back to sleep until early morning. Joseph later said I had a big smile on my face and was laughing, and I looked like a little child. Ah . . . Pra, my Love. It is so delicious to have a visit with you!

APPENDIX

Footnotes for Parts I, II, III, from
AWAKENING TO THE SACRED LOVE OF
THE TWIN FLAME

Copy of *The Ecstasy of Sacred Love*,
Message from Archangel Michael, LM-8-
2018. This monthly Archangel Michael
Message, originally published in 2006 and
republished in 2017, was channeled through
sacred scribe, Ronna Herman Vezane, who
has been a messenger on Earth for the
Archangel for many years. Her website is
www.starquestmastery.com. The Messages
appear online and are distributed to a
mailing list.

Copy of *The SoulMate Dispensation*, from
The Messages from God by Yael and Doug
Powell at Circle of Light and published in
*Eternal Twin Flame Love, The Story of
ShannaPra* in 2006.

Complete listing of all publications from
ARCHANGEL MICHAEL, ** STAR * QUEST
** BOOKS AND WISDOM TEACHINGS OF
LOVE AND INSPIRATION FROM
ARCHANGEL MICHAEL * RONNA / SACRED
SCRIBE found at www.starquestmastery.com

About the Author, Shanna MacLean

PART ONE FOOTNOTES

(1)   Messages from Archangel Michael, LM-8-2018, Ronna/Sacred Scribe. *The Ecstasy of Sacred Love.* This monthly Archangel Michael Message, originally published in 2006 and republished in 2017, was channeled through deeply respected scribe, Ronna (Herman) Vezane who has been a messenger on Earth for the Archangel for many years. www.starquestmastery.com. The Archangel Michael Messages appear online and are distributed each month to a mailing list.

(2)   The SoulMate Dispensation, published in *Say "Yes" to Love, God Explains SoulMates*, through Yael and Doug Powell, Circle of Light Press, 2001, pp. 9-11.

(3)   A copy of the full Archangel Michael Message, *The Ecstasy of Sacred Love,* may be found in this book's Appendix.

(4)   Segments of this section of this book were previously published in *Eternal Twin Flame*

46 I AWAKENING TO THE SACRED LOVE

Love, The Story of ShannaPra, Circle of
Light Press, copyright 2006 by Shanna
MacLean. The material quoted here is from
my actual, original notebook in which I
captured the experiences at the time they
occurred, thereby recording the Twin Flame
visits with authenticity.

(5) Highly recommended for spiritual study. The
list of Archangel Michael publications
through Ronna Herman Vezane appears in
the Appendix.

(6) Messages from God, *SoulMates, The Big
Picture*, through Yael and Doug Powell,
Circle of Light, unpublished, archived,
August 13, 2000, p. 10 of draft.

(7) The StarGate had been mentioned several
times in the Messages from God through
Yael. A depiction of the Stargate is on the
cover of the book, "Say YES to Love, God
Unveils Soulmate Love and Sacred
Sexuality.

(8) The paragraphs which follow, rather than
being from my initial typed notes when I
first met Pra, are copied from my first book,
*Eternal Twin Flame Love, The Story of
ShannaPra*, published in 2006 by Circle of
Light Press, copyright Shanna MacLean.

They were written at the time the events occurred with the intent of accuracy in the moment. Though very personal in content, I share all of these experiences that brothers and sisters on Earth may open to similar experiences with their Twin Flames. See *Eternal Twin Flame Love*, pp. 165-172.

(9) Message from God, *Sacred Sexuality: Creating Love in All Dimensions*, through Yael and Doug Powell, Circle of Light. Archived, June 6, 2001. Page 26 of draft.

(10) A translation of *ménage a trois* is: household for three or threesome.

PART TWO FOOTNOTES

(1) Messages from Archangel Michael, LM-8-2018, Ronna/Sacred Scribe. *The Ecstasy of Sacred Love*, monthly email, p. 2.

(2) *The Seven Sacred Rays*, Aurelia Louise Jones, Mount Shasta Light Publishing, 2007, pp. 41-42.

(3) A Note About My Communication with Pra: Since my personal communication with Pra is mostly telepathic or in pictures or feelings,

and only infrequently in words, I have called upon the services of a beloved friend to assist with the interviews with Pra within this book. This is a sister who has a beautiful gift of ease of communication with the spirit world and is able to easily place words upon Pra's messages. This wonderful friend and I met years ago when she came to a workshop at Circle of Light. In our very first conversation, she said, "I can communicate with your Pra!" Thus, began a deep friendship. She prefers to remain anonymous here, but she offers her services to support LightWorkers in phone sessions as a spiritual counselor. You may make contact with her through me if you desire.

(4) My main sources for the excerpted information that follows, from which I will quote liberally, are: (a) *Say YES to Love, God Explains SoulMates; (b) Say Yes to Love, God Unveils SoulMate Love and Sacred Sexuality,* both through Yael and Doug Powell, Circle of Light, 2002, Circle of Light Press. These books are in the process of being reprinted. It may be difficult to find a new copy at this time; one can try all of the used bookstores. The Messages from God in these books still contain, in my opinion, the most detailed and powerful information on

Twin Flames available to us, communicated directly from Source through an elevated, advanced soul, Yael Powell; (b) Two unpublished Messages from God, archived in the Circle of Light notebooks: *SoulMates, The Big Picture; It Is Giving, Not Receiving That Reveals The SoulMate;* about the human journey, documenting parallel and similar teachings given by Archangel Michael throughout Ronna's many books.

(5) All material directly quoted from the Messages from God comes from *Say YES to Love, God Unveils SoulMate Love and Sacred Sexuality*, or from the two unpublished Messages from God mentioned in (4).

PART THREE FOOTNOTES

(1) Since my personal communication with Pra is mostly telepathic or in pictures or feelings, and only infrequently in words, I have called upon a beloved friend to assist with the language in the dialogues with Pra within this book. This is a sister who has a beautiful gift of ease of communication with the spirit world and is able to easily assist

me in placing words upon Pra's messages.
This wonderful friend and I met years ago
when she came to a workshop at Circle of
Light. In our very first conversation, she
said, "I am in communication with your
Pra!" Thus, began a deep lifelong friendship.
She prefers to remain anonymous here, but
she offers her services as a spiritual
counselor to support LightWorkers in
telephone sessions. You may make contact
with her through me.

MESSAGES FROM ARCHANGEL MICHAEL * LM-8-2018
RONNA VEZANE/ SACRED SCRIBE
THE ECSTASY OF SACRED LOVE

Beloved masters, we ask you to pause for a moment and turn inward as you quickly move into your Sacred Heart Center. Take a deep breath and tap into your Sacred Mind Center as well, where your higher frequency Memory Seed Atoms are stored. Now ponder these questions: What is it that you yearn for above all things? What is missing from your life that affects everything you think, feel and do? The answer is: Sacred Love, dear hearts.

We do not mean love as you now experience it in the physical realm, but the Sacred Love of your Twin Flame; your Soul family in the higher realms; your wondrous angelic friends; the great Beings of Light; our Father/Mother God, and the Supreme Creator. That is what is missing. That is what you have yearned for ever since you left your lofty home among the stars, and before you divided yourself into two Sparks of individualized awareness—one masculine Spark and one feminine Spark of Divine consciousness—so that you could reflect and experience the glory and diversity of our

Father/Mother God.

In the past, we have explained how you agreed to separate from your sacred partner in order to fulfill your Divine mission, and how you have taken turns in assuming a masculine or feminine body. And how, most often, one of you stayed in the higher realms while the other incarnated in the physical expression. Rarely were you given an opportunity to meet in the physical world; however, there were wondrous times in the higher dimensions when you were allowed to join together for a time of joyous reunion; for an infusion of loving ecstasy, a blending of your Essence, a remembrance of what you left behind , and what you have to look forward to in the future. This wondrous gift has not been available to you since you sank into the density of the Third/Fourth Dimensional expression—UNTIL NOW.

We have asked much of you over these past years of awakening, and you have suffered through many trials and tests. We see that great multitudes of you have slowly, but diligently, changed for the better as you lifted and harmonized your frequency patterns and let go of old, self-limiting thought forms and limitations. You have relinquished most of your ego-driven emotions and habits, as you have striven to return to center within your Sacred Heart and become a Self-master. We have watched you struggle to understand all the new, mindboggling concepts, as you endeavor to claim and live your truth to the best of your ability. We salute and honor you for your dedication and your constant vigilance in monitoring your thoughts, and for always striving for the "greatest good of all."

In reviewing the past, have you not changed radically for the better? Isn't your personal world more tranquil and filled with joy? Are you not gaining proficiency in creating abundance and the things you desire to live in comfort and safety? Have you learned and taken to heart the universal laws of prosperity, whereby, you affirm that you are entitled to abundance in all things? Remember, you must keep the universal flow circulating. You are to take what you need, and then allow the balance to flow out into the world to be shared, so that it can be replenished and multiplied, over and over again.

Yes, you have been reaping many rewards for your dedication and loyalty, and we are most gratified with the progress you, the Seekers of Light, have made. However, the gains you have made and the miracles you have experienced in the past are nothing compared to what is now available and awaiting you: a gift beyond compare.

We have spoken much about the purity of

unconditional love, which was encoded within your Adam/Eve Kadmon Light Body, as you journeyed forth as emissaries for our Father/Mother God. And how it became distorted by the physical, ego desire-body as you sank into the density and the broader spectrum of duality in the Third/Fourth—Dimensional experience. It was not ordained that you should lose touch with the Sacred Love of our Father/Mother God and the Creator, just as it was not planned for you to forget your lineage and your Divine heritage.

As you began your journey into the density of the Third and Fourth Dimensions, the veil of forgetfulness was placed over your memory. It was not meant as a punishment, but an act of mercy, for it would have been overwhelmingly painful to remember the negativity of your past incarnations, as well as very confusing to have access to your many experiences in the higher realms of consciousness. Remember, in most of your past incarnations in the physical realm, you brought very little of your God consciousness with you, and the majority of human Beings have been functioning within the lower frequency levels of brain consciousness.

That has now changed, as we have explained in the past, no matter where you chose to incarnate on the spectrum of Light and shadow in this lifetime, it is not where you belong. You chose your family lineage, your physical vessel, and the circumstances of your life. For it was decided—with the help of your angelic guides and guardian angels—what the best overall experiences would be to assist you to heal old negative thought patterns and to resolve ancient karmic issues, in order to return to balance and harmony and attain self-mastery once more.

We have told you that you have encoded within your DNA and Divine blueprint all the virtues, attributes, qualities and aspects of our Father/Mother God. You are an electromagnetic force field; an energetic package of Divine Light substance. Encoded within each of you is the ecstasy and bliss of Sacred Love, a cosmic, orgasmic experience beyond anything you can imagine in the physical expression. Opening and attuning to the physical, Sacred Heart center is just the beginning. It prepares you for the multilevel reunification process whereby you gradually reconnect with the many Facets of your Self. Many of you are now comfortable with the concept of communing with us, your unseen friends and companions of the higher realms. Now, a most wondrous gift is being offered to you, the ability to reconnect with your Twin Flame, and to experience the ecstasy of Sacred Love. No longer do you have to feel lonely or hunger for loving acceptance and validation of your worthiness. No longer do you have to yearn for fulfillment, and desire someone in the physical to reflect back to you your beauty or give you a sense of belonging.

Our Father/Mother God have been waiting for the time when they can offer you this gift beyond compare. When we speak of returning to Oneness, we mean that in the greatest sense, as well as in the many subtle levels of integration in the physical realm. We have told you that the Divine blueprint for the future is now in place, and many rules and conditions of the past will no longer apply to those of you firmly on the path of heightened awareness. No longer will you incarnate with one of the three major God Rays as your predominate godly overlay, but you will have all twelve Rays of galactic consciousness fully available and active. In the future, it will be up to you to decide which Rays and combination of Rays you wish to focus on, develop and master. Many of you will choose to not return to planet Earth but will join with your Twin Flame and many members of your Soul family, as you accept a new Divine mission in order to assist in the creation of the new Golden Galaxy of the future. Many rules, conditions and concepts of your earthly experiences are changing as you evolve from human beings to Galactic Beings, in the process of returning to your true estate as a master in the realms of Light.

How do you go about connecting with your Twin Flame? First you must say "YES TO SACRED LOVE." You must desire this connection with all your Being. You must open your mind and heart to the concept that you have a Twin Flame, and that it is possible to reconnect with them. Go into your Pyramid of Light and lie on the crystal table, move into your Sacred Heart Center, and allow the Sacred Love/Light of our Mother/Father God and the Creator to pour forth and fill you to overflowing. Send out the call to your Twin Flame and ask them to join with you. Speak the words of love that fill your heart and mind, and then listen for an answer. Know that you will receive an answer; however, do not put any conditions as to how and when it will happen. Just know that when the time is right, your beloved will appear—in some way or in some form. Your reconnection in Spirit form will be a very "personal happening," unique and precious to you and your beloved.

Open your heart to all the possibilities of Sacred Love and know that it is your Divine birthright to experience this most intimate gift. You do not have to share your experiences with others but know that those around you will begin to feel the difference in you, and will respond to your uplifted, loving nature. Everyone around you will benefit from your expressions of Sacred Love.

Even if you already have a mate or companion in the physical expression, it is permissible and desirable to reconnect with your Divine counterpart in spirit form. As you connect with and integrate the attributes and qualities of your other half, something magical happens: You return to wholeness within your own Being, and you no longer look outside yourself for validation or for what you feel is missing. It is the quickest and surest way to feel and then learn to express unconditional love; therefore, your frequency patterns will be lifted, and you will begin to radiate that refined love to your mate, your loved ones and everyone around you. Most often, your mate and your family will respond to your emanations of Sacred, unconditional love, and the interactions between you will quickly change for the better.

Many dear Souls have agreed at a Soul level to journey alone during this lifetime, or to focus on their spiritual mission instead of seeking a mate or a close companion. We tell you, you do not have to complete your earthly journey alone, nor do you have to wait until you transcend to experience the "state of bliss" of the higher realms. It is time for you to shed the filters and veils that have been placed over your memory and consciousness. It is time for you to remember who you are, and ALL that you are. It is a time of reunification of the highest order.

A small minority of Twin Flames may be incarnated on Earth at the same time, and it is sometimes ordained that they will find each other and make a connection. In such an instance, both halves of the whole agreed to incarnate at the same time to see how Twin Flames would progress together in the physical expression. Unless the two people involved are firmly on the path and are fairly balanced within, these unions do not result in the bliss state, but bring more strife and unhappiness into their lives. There is often an obsession with each other which results in a "can't live with, but can't live without" situation, for they have not learned the secret of Sacred Love, and they are still playing the game of duality and ego-driven love with many conditions.

Going into your Pyramid of Light in the Fifth Dimension has prepared you for new levels of awareness, and the many gifts of en-LIGHTEN-ment that await you in the future. The Cities of Light meditation has also accelerated the process of preparing you for the reunion and rejoining with your Twin Flame, and also with many Fragments of yourself that you left behind in the higher realms.

Many of you will experience doubt, and perhaps some negative emotions regarding this concept of Twin Flame reunion, and the possibility of cosmic, orgasmic bliss. We tell you, beloveds, the feelings of love and the orgasmic union in the physical body pales in comparison to the bliss and the ecstasy we experience in the higher realms. We are in a constant state of bliss, but the most precious gift of all is when we merge with our Divine compliment, blending our Essence and ALL of who and what we are. At each higher dimensional level, the blissful, ecstatic state of Sacred love is magnified. You, as humans, could not tolerate the power and magnificence of the Creator's Sacred Love that we experience constantly.

Are you willing to test this new level of cosmic awareness? Are you ready to accept this Divine gift that is being offered you? You have nothing to lose and everything to gain. Your Twin Flame is waiting for you to put out the call. When you say "YES to Sacred Love," you will feel a dramatic change in your Sacred Heart Center as it prepares to receive the rarified gift of Sacred Love sent forth from our Mother/Father God. Your earthly life will forever be changed. Call on us and we will guide and assist you in every way possible. Know that I am with you always and you are loved beyond measure, I AM Archangel

Michael. Transmitted through Ronna VEZANE*
STAR*QUEST. www.starquestmastery.com

THE SOULMATE DISPENSATION

"The SoulMate Dispensation", from The
Messages from God by Yael and Doug
Powell at Circle of Light (published in
*Eternal Twin Flame Love, The Story of
ShannaPra* in 2006.)

The SoulMate Dispensation is a magnificent gift
from God to humanity. It is a special
dispensation that allows SoulMates to come
together before they are in the perfected state of
pure Love that would be the requirement of the
natural law of resonance ("like attracts like").
This means that all on Earth now have access to
their SoulMate, their one Twin Flame, right
where they are in their path of awakening,
regardless of whether or not their resonance is
Love and only Love.

What this does is allow true Love to now be
made manifest in every person's life. The reason
for this dispensation is that once SoulMate Love
is experienced, this Love will then open each
person's heart, helping to clear away any
blockages that may have kept Love at a distance.

It will be the living proof that Love exists, and that God loves each of us so much that God's Love is and has always been embodies in our lives as our SoulMate.

It does not matter whether or not you understand what this means. It only matters that you put out the call in your heart for your SoulMate—that you say "Yes" each day to the opening of your heart to Love. What matters is that you know that the longing for Love you've always felt was placed there by God and was meant to keep you looking for reunion with your SoulMate, so you can live in Love, together, in the world.

NOTE: Please remember that the terms Twin Flame and SoulMate were used interchangeably in the Messages from God at Circle of Light Spiritual Center.

HIGHLY RECOMMENDED

These are the Wisdom Teachings of Love and
Inspiration from Archangel Michael through his
Sacred Scribe, Ronna Herman Vezane

** STAR * QUEST **

www.starquestmastery.com

** BOOKS **

BOOK ONE *ON WINGS OF LIGHT * ONLY
AVAILABLE AS AN E-BOOK * $15

BOOK TWO * THE GOLDEN PROMISE * 6 X 9
PAPERBACK * $18

BOOK THREE: YOUR SACRED QUEST© * 6 X 9
PAPERBACK * $22 ** E-BOOK * $15

BOOK FOUR: LET THERE BE LIGHT© * 6 X 9
PAPERBACK * $22

BOOK FIVE: REVEALED COSMIC TRUTHS© * 6 x
9 PAPERBACK * $25

BOOK SIX ** SECRETS OF SELF MASTERY© * 8 ½
X 11 SPIRAL- BOUND BOOK * $25

BOOK SEVEN ** THE MAGIC AND MAJESTY OF

ASCENDING HUMANITY© * 8 ½ X 11 SPIRAL-BOUND BOOK * $25

CO-AUTHORED: KEVIN ADAM & RONNA VEZANE: OUR INFINITE POWER© * 6 X 9 PAPERBACK * $25 ** E-BOOK: $15

CO-AUTHORED: KEVIN ADAM & RONNA VEZANE * UNIFIED CREATOR SPIRITUALITY© * 6 X 9 PAPERBACK * $25 ** E-BOOK: 15

STUDY MANUALS

SCRIPTING YOUR DESTINY ©* 6 X 9 SOFT COVER PAPERBACK ** $25 ** E-BOOK: 15

REFERENCE & REVELATIONS © * 8 ½ X 11 SPIRAL-BOUND BOOK * $20 ** E-BOOK: $15

OPENING TO CHANNEL * DEVELOPING YOUR TELEPATHIC COMMUNICATION SKILLS© *8 X 11 * SPIRAL-BOUND BOOK * $20 ** E-BOOK: $15

SYMPTOMS OF ASCENSION© ** 8 ½ X 11 SPIRAL-BOUND BOOKLET * $11

ACTIVATING THE MEMORY SEED ATOMS OF THE FUTURE© ** E-BOOK * $15

A METAFICTION TRILOGY BY RONNA VEZANE:

ONCE UPON A NEW WORLD© 6 X 9 SOFT COVER
PAPER BACK: $9.77 EACH OR $25.00 FOR THE
SET

** ONCE UPON A NEW WORLD© is a series of
six stories I choose to call "metafiction." The
stories are about MY journey (incarnations) as a
SPARK of the GOD FORCE, and its evolution
through time and space.

ABOUT THE AUTHOR

SHANNA MACLEAN

My life in this incarnation on planet Earth has been an unending kaleidoscope of activity. I entered via a loving mother who was unable to keep me and was fortunately adopted at two weeks. My musical and academic talents emerged early. Despite many financial and family challenges, my adoptive mother insisted on an excellent education for me, placing me in private first grade at four years old and at the same time, starting me with private piano lessons. I graduated from Brockton (MA) High School at sixteen years old and graduated *cum laude* from Smith College at twenty. I later added Masters Degrees in Music and in Counseling that allowed me active careers— teaching music at the college level, positions as an arts administrator and as a counselor for elementary age children in the public school system. Writing and editing have been more recent professional pathways.

Born, raised and educated in Massachusetts, I have also lived in Washington, D.C., California, Washington State, Maine, North Carolina, Arkansas and more than anywhere else, in New Mexico. Three marriages each brought gifts— experiences in the political world, a home full of music, and extensive international travel and residence in foreign countries (Indonesia, Colombia and Chile). I have three children and six grandchildren. I currently reside, for the second time, in Santa Fe, New Mexico, with my partner, Joseph, and our precious cat, Lotus, in a beautiful rural area, La Cienega, south of the city.

The centerpiece of this diverse life was definitely my twelve years at Circle of Light Spiritual Center (2001-2012). My role there as the anchor for administrative needs included managing the office (including the wedding business), transcribing and editing the Messages from God, managing the publication of books, designing websites and organizing workshops for people from all over the world. It was the most expansive, fulfilling and gratifying of all my professional and personal experiences. Every skill I had ever acquired was fully utilized during this time, even my music composition and definitely my counseling training. Every question I had ever pondered about who we truly are and about life on Earth was lovingly answered through the Messages from God that flowed every day through Yael Powell and were the purpose for Circle of Light's existence. That time in my life brought my blessed connection with my Twin Flame, Pra, which resulted in a first book, *Eternal TwinFlame Love, The Story of ShannaPra* and now, the volume you hold in your hands.

I continue to live and share the Messages from God extensively and with this book, fulfill my promise to be a part of bringing forth the life changing information about Twin Flames that we were given at Circle of Light. I can only say the most profound THANK YOU in my heart to our beloved Creator for my life experiences, for the spiritual awakening of this lifetime and for the honor and privilege of being a messenger for others.

I would be delighted to hear from you at:

ShannaPra@gmail.com

TwinFlamesShannaPra.com